Ways That Work

Ways That Work

Putting Social Studies Standards into Practice

Tarry Lindquist

HEINEMANN ◆ Portsmouth, NH

Heinemann
A division of Reed Elsevier Inc.
361 Hanover Street
Portsmouth, NH 03801-3912

Offices and agents throughout the world

The author and publisher wish to thank those who have generously given permission
to reprint borrowed material:

"The 'Bubble' Classroom" from *Aviation for the Elementary Level*. Copyright © 1990
by Raytheon Aircraft Company. Reprinted by permission.

Excerpts from "Constitutional Visions", *The Bill of Rights for Upper Elementary and Middle School
Students*. Copyright © 1992 by ICEL. Reprinted by permission of Margaret Fisher, Director.

Excerpts adapted from "Social Studies Now" by Tarry Lindquist in *Instructor*,
November/December 1996. Copyright © 1996 by Scholastic Inc. Reproduced by permission.

Excerpts from *Expectations of Excellence: Curriculum Standards for Social Studies*, National Council for
the Social Studies (Washington, DC, 1994). Reprinted by permission. Further information
about the social studies standards can be obtained from National Council for the Social Studies,
3501 Newark Street, N.W., Washington, DC 20016;
tel. (202) 966-7840, fax: (202) 966-2061; e-mail: publications@ncss.org

Appendix 2-3: Directions for "Little" Book reprinted by permission of Tarry Lindquist: *Seeing the Whole
Through Social Studies* (Heinemann, A division of Reed Elsevier Inc., Portsmouth, NH, 1995).

Library of Congress Cataloging-in-Publication Data

Lindquist, Tarry.
Ways that work : putting social studies standards into practice /
Tarry Lindquist.
p.   cm.
Includes bibliographical references.
ISBN 0-435-08907-2
1. Social sciences—Study and teaching (Elementary)—United
States—Curricula.   2. Social sciences—Study and teaching
(Secondary)—United States—Curricula.   3. Social sciences—Study
and teaching—Standards—United States.   I. Title.
LB1584.L545   1997
300'.71—dc21   97-30027
                                                            CIP

Acquiring editor: William Varner
Production editors: Renée Nicholls and Elizabeth Valway
Cover illustration: Monika Kasina
Photographs: Judi Slepyan
Cover designer: Joni Doherty
Manufacturing coordinator: Louise Richardson

Printed in the United States of America on acid-free paper

01 00   RRD   6

To our first grandchild, Taylor Katharine.
May she walk in wisdom and beauty.

Contents

Preface

Welcome to *Ways That Work: Putting Social Studies Standards into Practice*. This book is my response to three recent catalysts: (1) my three-year participation on our local school district's social studies curriculum team, (2) our youngest daughter's having recently earned a teaching certificate, and (3) current use of national standards.

New Expectations

Let's begin with the first. Charged with the responsibility to articulate our K–12 social studies curriculum while attending to new state-mandated standards, our curriculum team has struggled to meet two very different sets of needs. On the one hand, after years of not hiring a soul, we have teachers brand-new to the district. They want to know what it is they are supposed to teach, how much of it they are supposed to teach, and how they will know when they are done. They also want to know what resources to use to accomplish their goals. On the other hand, we have seasoned educators who have been teaching their favorite units for years. The way these curricular units have been articulated is more akin to oral history than written record. Because of recent state and national mandates, these veterans now have to exchange familiar approaches for new content and goals that are driven by forces outside their classrooms.

The formal definition of social studies is challenging:

Social studies is the integrated study of the social sciences and humanities to promote civic competence. Within the school program, social studies provides coordinated, systematic study drawing upon such disciplines as anthropology, archaeology, economics, geography, history, law, philosophy, political science, psychology, religion, sociology, as well as appropriate content from the humanities, mathematics, and natural sciences. The primary purpose of social studies is to help young people develop the ability to make informed and reasoned decisions for the public good as citizens of a culturally diverse, democratic society in an interdependent world. (NCSS)

While most of us have had experiences both as students and as adults with different math disciplines (geometry and algebra, for example), many teachers do not feel they have enough background to teach social studies well because it is so multidisciplinary. Many experienced teachers rely on textbooks to teach social studies. In fact, in many districts, the text is the curriculum. While this is not necessarily bad, our social studies curriculum team decided that textbooks will not be the *sole* resource for learning social studies in our district. We are committed to bringing a more holistic curriculum to our students, to encouraging and supporting teachers in the development of integrated units of study, and to providing students with the opportunity to experience the full range of social studies knowledge, skills, and attitudes. This book is a resource for teachers new to teaching beyond the text: I think they know lots more than they give themselves credit for, and *Ways That Work: Putting Social Studies Standards into Practice* affirms strategies they are already using in other content areas, confirms ideas they are thinking of, reminds them about things they used to do, and suggests new ways they might like to try.

New Teachers

The second event is much more personal. Our daughter Tani just completed her student teaching. She received a liberal arts degree five years ago but she recently completed a master's degree in education and has just become the twentieth member of our family to teach in the state of Washington. During her student teaching, I watched her work hard to pull together lessons of substance and interest. As with most student teachers, some of them worked and some of them didn't.

Now in her own classroom, Tani has to manage behavior, plan content for her diverse student population, and meet individual needs as well as a set of state Educational Academic Learning Requirements for every subject while tuning in to local and national standards in math, language arts, science, and social studies. Much of her time is spent trying to incorporate all the skills these outside mandates say she should be teaching within the reality of the school day, given the population she's working with, and using the available resources. Priorities, established mainly by the kinds of standardized testing being carried out across our nation, tend to be reading, writing, and arithmetic. By the time she's dealt with the traditional three R's, there's not a lot of time left in which to create meaningful social studies lessons.

Ways That Work is written for her and for the many new teachers who enter our profession each year. It includes sample units for the national social studies standards and features strategies that work across the curriculum so that novices can extrapolate what they need to create powerful social studies for their students quickly and effectively.

Reaction to Reform

The third event that inspired this book is what has happened across this nation since the national standards were published in the major disciplines. Teachers and schools are being besieged by wide-ranging interpretations of the reform movement. What began as an effort to codify educational goals nationally and to help teachers assess both students and themselves has turned, in many states, into yet another whip with which to flog education and educators. Some politicians, the press, and some parents are using reform as an excuse to launch initiatives that destroy the public's confidence in our schools. Equally distressing, many standards are being reduced to pencil and paper tests that once again try to fit all students into exactly the same size hole. Gone are the words "developmentally appropriate." Vanished is the concept of "holistic education." One size fits all and it's called "basic."

So what do we do about it? Many teachers and their administrators are reacting to this new bludgeoning by turning to less integrated, more regulated kinds of teaching. Many school districts are once again searching for a single magical way to reassure their critics. Their search often ends in restrictive educational practices that encourage unidimensional teaching.

However, that's not an answer that will be successful with our students. Research tells us that "organizing instruction into broad, thematically based clusters of work through which reading, writing, and speaking activities are interrelated promotes understanding of the connections among activities and ideas" (Cawelti 1995, 76). Rather than "back to basics," I would like to see us move "forward to balance." I am convinced a balanced program, one that deliberately integrates language arts, literature, and social studies, as well as other disciplines, provides more opportunities for our students to experience success in learning. Currently, students spend 60 percent of their school time developing competencies in reading, writing, and oral language. Let's give them something of substance to read, write, and talk about. *Ways That Work* is a collection of ideas about how social studies and language arts can be combined to promote learning and to create an active, informed citizenship for the twenty-first century.

Acknowledgments

No book about teaching and learning is the result of a single person's work. Rather, such a book captures the energy of many people. Like taking a snapshot, the author may still a moment, stay an experience, or reflect on the significance of an event, but it is the people who touch the author's life that make this kind of book possible. Thank you all.

To the Paradise Island classes of 2001, 2002, 2003, 2004, and 2005 who tried the ways, taught me what worked, and cheerfully had their pictures taken time and time again.

To Judi Slepyan, who took the photographs that reflect my students', as well as her own, talent, humor, and goodness.

To Paula Christoulis, Pat Desimone, and Mike Halverson, Nancy Kezner, Frank Perry, and Carole Muth, my fourth- and fifth-grade colleagues at Lakeridge Elementary who continue to share, learn, and laugh with me.

To my principal and friend, John Cameron, who continues to encourage me to try new things and explore new territories.

To Kathy Morrison, our principal-intern who meets every crisis with a song and a smile.

To Azizi Amundsen, the best sub and friend a teacher ever had, who keeps our intermediate classes at Lakeridge going when we are gone.

To our daughter Tani, who is teaching three doors down from me and who enriches the profession.

To our daughter Tia and son-in-law Scott, who have given us a precious gift, the next generation of teachers.

To my good friends and social studies colleagues, Marte Peet, Oralee Kramer, Rick Moulden, and Marj Montgomery, who continue to share ideas, resources, and knowledge and are the best of traveling companions.

To the colleagues I meet when I speak around North America who share the vision of a peaceful classroom where head, hands, heart, and a touch of humor help all children learn.

To the team at Heinemann, who made the whole book come together so effectively: Bill Varner, Alan Huisman, Renée Nicholls, and Elizabeth Valway.

Finally, to my husband, Malcolm. No one writes a book in a year and teaches full-time without incredible support. Thank you, Mr. Incredible.

Introduction

Why Social Studies Standards

Why do I choose the national standards for social studies, rather than those for history, geography, economics, or civics to use in my classroom? The social studies standards are a better fit with overall curriculum concerns and describe student performance with a more comprehensive focus. The individual discipline standards, such as history and economics, focus primarily on content. On the other hand, the social studies standards blend what to teach with how to teach.

In elementary grades, students are still learning how to learn. Content acquisition should be balanced with essential skill development. These skills include (1) the acquisition of information, (2) the manipulation of data, (3) the construction of knowledge, (4) the ability to take and support a position on an issue, identify a problem and propose a solution, or recount a story, and (5) the ability to work individually or in groups.

Finding the Time

The most precious gift we can give our students is time to read from many books, time to research questions, time to wrestle with conflicting interpretations, time to wander through divergent paths of social studies, and time to revisit previous questions in a new context. Yet in today's overcrowded classrooms, time is one of the least available commodities we have.

Integrated Skills

Integrating skills is one way I gain time in my classroom. I no longer have a language arts period. Instead my students learn and apply language arts skills through social studies. For example, they write personal letters to a historical person of note, such as Abraham Lincoln after reading a biography about him. They tell Mr. Lincoln the reason for their admiration and how they think he would react to society today. Or they write to me, comparing two similar assignments, contrasting what they did, detailing what they'd change, and choosing their favorite of the two based on their own criteria.

When my students give a persuasive speech, they speak about issues we have studied in social studies, such as planks in the recent presidential campaigns including ways to protect the environment, government involvement in health care, and how to reform schools.

They apply thinking skills as they create Venn diagrams comparing the pioneers' journey from St. Louis to Oregon with what the journey might entail today. Organizational strategies, grammar, and writing skills are all approached, applied, and extended through social studies content. What better way to give our students something to write about, think about, and care about?

A Flexible Schedule

When I started teaching, my schedule was like a clock. If it was two o'clock on Tuesday, we must be learning social studies. Now I have a much more flexible schedule. Instead of a science period, a social studies period, and a language arts period, I have identified a major part of each day as "block." Block period gives us the time to explore the many points of view regarding the Civil War or the obstacles to moving west. Later in the year, block period is when we investigate our local watershed and research water quality. Science and social studies are not tidy little subjects that we open two times a week after we finish language arts and math. Instead, most of the day revolves around major themes from our social studies or science curriculum. I explain this plan to promote depth rather than coverage of material to the parents of my students early in the fall, and so far I have had their full support and my principal's as well.

However, during the times I'm focusing on science I keep a thread of social studies going by finding a number of books that discuss the related historical periods. Sometimes I require all my students to read specific books. Sometimes I encourage them to choose from the collection I've identified.

Peak Experiences

Finally, I integrate processes, skills, and knowledge across the curriculum through a culminating project or "peak experience." This is an activity that requires students to apply their newly acquired knowledge and skills in a way they will remember. It isn't a textbook read nor a paper-and-pencil test taken because the school district or the state requires it. These are magical, memorable moments, later recalled at class reunions ("I'll never forget . . .") or retold by parents as parables to their children ("When I was your age . . ."), that bring diverse students together for a moment of shared accomplishment and provide a springboard for similar working relationships in the future. Sometimes the peak experience bubbles up from the interests and ideas of the students. Sometimes I assign it. It is often a play, a presentation, a reenactment, a fair, a performance, an exhibit, or a demonstration that captures excellence in learning. It is also a venue for authentic assessment. Each chapter in *Ways That Work* highlights at least one peak experience.

Getting There Is Where It's At

Studying history, geography, or any of the social sciences in the elementary classroom is more a journey than a destination. How kids learn social studies is as important as what they learn. In the social studies–centered classroom, how they acquire the information is as significant as the information they find. We need to permit our students to end a unit of study with questions, perhaps with more questions than when we began. Social studies is the ongoing pursuit not only of What happened? but of Who said? and What was their point of view?

Multiple Intelligences

Basing classroom strategies on the theory of multiple intelligences is a good way to help kids demonstrate what they know. Dr. Howard Gardner, a Harvard psychologist, developed this theory more than ten years ago, and teachers are now putting his ideas into practice in classrooms across America.

Here's a quick checklist of the multiple intelligences Gardner identified. He believes that *all* students have the capacity to develop *each* intelligence. I agree with him and make sure my kids have lots of opportunities to experience each intelligence and to practice being smart in all seven.

- *Linguistic intelligence* centers on language. I use this intelligence when I give kids an opportunity to work with books, develop rich vocabularies, and to express themselves through discussion, drama, debate, or writing.
- *Interpersonal intelligence* centers on social interaction. My students apply this intelligence by engaging in group work, cooperating with others to produce a shared product, or helping others.
- *Intrapersonal intelligence* centers on working independently and quietly. I schedule time during which my students can process feelings, make assignments that require thoughtful responses, and encourage self-direction. There is "alone" time in my classroom every day.
- *Visual-spatial intelligence* centers on images, photographs, graphs, charts, diagrams, and artwork. Here's an opportunity to provide lots of visual stimulation and allow for unique solutions and non-traditional approaches to problem solving.
- *Kinesthetic intelligence* centers on moving, touching, and doing. I structure my classroom day to encourage short movement breaks,

plan lots of hands-on activities, and create active, student-centered simulations.

- *Logical-mathematical intelligence* centers on forming concepts and finding patterns and relationships. I consistently provide sequential organizational structures, encourage questions, and incorporate games, kits, and puzzles throughout social studies units.
- *Musical intelligence* centers on rhythm, melody, and pitch. Providing music to listen to, instruments to play, and opportunities to sing, clap, or tap out information in class, and honoring student work that primarily uses music are some of the ways I incorporate this intelligence in my classroom.

About This Book

This is an "idea book" that blends national social studies standards with effective teaching strategies for teachers new to the profession, new to the upper elementary classroom, or new to teaching beyond the textbook. Its value increases as you personalize it. I encourage you to examine the structure of each unit and then insert your own content into the ones that are most appropriate or most appealing. You'll want to add your own "spices" to reflect your personality and your students' needs and to exchange "ingredients" to use the resources at hand. For instance, in the first chapter, I describe a cooperative unit based on student-centered research. I use the theme of westward expansion. The same unit structure works equally well with topics such as the Civil War or Canada and with broader conceptual approaches such as interdependence or change.

I don't teach all these units in one year. Some years I teach several. Some years, fewer. My decisions about which to teach are influenced by my students, the focus of my school district, the concerns of my community, and current issues on the national level.

I also didn't create these units in one year. Some have been in the making for almost a decade. Each unit changes as new materials become available, as my students grow, as I become more informed about content and the way children learn.

Each chapter models a different way of organizing social studies learning, addressing different social studies standards, and concentrating on different student skills. The chapters each include multidisciplinary strategies, suggest a variety of assessment techniques, and integrate language arts and literature. Annotated bibliographies are provided. Together, the chapters illustrate that there is no one way to teach social studies. Indeed, the magic of teaching social studies lies in the richness of the available content, the variety of strategies to choose from, and the diversity of viewpoints to explore.

A quick reference follows listing the national standard(s), the social studies goals, and the essential skills in each chapter. Also listed are the disciplines integrated in each unit, the specific teaching strategies introduced, and the assessment strategies used.

Chapter 1: By the Book: Learning History Beyond the Text

Standard:	Time, continuity, and change
Goal:	Enrich historical knowledge and enjoyment of history while demonstrating the ability to sift fact from fiction
Skills:	Comprehend what is read; recognize and understand an increasing number of social studies terms; locate information from a variety of resources; compile, organize, and evaluate information; draw conclusions or inferences from evidence; express personal convictions
Strategies:	Walking in Their Shoes interviews and video books, human opinion continuum, cooperative units
Disciplines:	History, reading, language arts, and art
Assessment:	Peer evaluation

Chapter 2: A Place at the Table: Investigating Global Issues in a Day

Standard:	Global connections

Goal:	Demonstrate understanding of issues related to universal human rights; explore the causes, consequences, and possible solutions to persistent, contemporary, and emerging global issues
Skills:	Use information from a variety of resources; extract and interpret information; communicate orally and in writing; draw conclusions; make decisions and act on those decisions
Strategies:	Wondershape, opinion poll, accordion book
Disciplines:	Global studies, geography, health, math, language arts
Assessment:	Student reflection

Chapter 3: Across the United States: Creating a Collegial Classroom Community

Standard:	People, places, and environment
Goal:	Create mental and physical maps of locales and regions that demonstrate understanding of relative location, direction, size, and shape; identify examples of how environment shapes culture
Skills:	Extract and interpret information; see things from the point of view of others; adjust own behavior to fit the dynamics of various groups and situations; assist in setting goals for the group; participate in persuading, compromising, debating, and negotiating in the resolutions of conflicts and differences
Strategies:	Little books of alliteration, storyboards, pictorial maps, posters, research writing, mock governor's speeches, parade of states, states fair
Disciplines:	Geography, reading, language arts, art
Assessment:	Student rubrics, teacher-student evaluation

Chapter 4: Trade Fair: Orchestrating a One-Period Peak Experience

Standard: Production, distribution, and consumption

Goal: Explore and demonstrate the relationship of cost to supply and demand

Skills: Plan; consider the consequences of decision-making; make generalizations

Strategies: Simulation, quartiles

Disciplines: Economics, language arts

Assessment: Reflective self-assessment

Chapter 5: Cooperative Biographies: Focusing on Reading, Research, Writing, and Responsibility

Standard: Individual development and identity

Goal: Develop an understanding and appreciation for our American heritage

Skills: Locate information from a variety of resources; extract and interpret information; communicate in writing; apply technical skills; contribute to the development of a supportive climate in groups; participate in making rules and guidelines for group life; serve as a leader or a follower; participate in delegating duties, organizing, planning, making decisions, and taking action in group settings

Strategies: Cooperative biographies, fact flip board

Disciplines: History, psychology, language arts, reading

Assessment: Observation checklist

Chapter 6: Bridges to Other Cultures: Infusing Cultural Studies Across the Curriculum

Standard: Culture

Goal: Compare similarities and differences in the ways cultures meet human needs and concerns

Skills:	Compare things, ideas, events, and situations on the basis of similarities and differences; draw conclusions or inferences from evidence; arrive at general ideas; understand one's own beliefs, feelings, abilities, and shortcomings and how they affect relationships with others
Strategies:	Chinese shadow puppets, Japanese story cards (*kamishibai*), Native American time ball
Disciplines:	Geography, history, sociology, anthropology, reading, language arts, art
Assessment:	Inventory

Chapter 7: Constitutional Visions: Connecting the Constitution, Kids, Science, Civics, and Social Studies

Standards:	Power, authority, and governance
	Individuals, groups, and institutions
	Science, technology, and society
	Civic ideals and practices
Goal:	Understand and appreciate the historical development of structures and functions of power, authority and governance in America; learn how institutions are formed; explore how technology and science support diverse lifestyles; develop civic ideals and practice civic participation
Skills:	Group data in categories according to appropriate criteria; note cause and effect relationships; combine critical concepts into a statement of conclusions based on information; reinterpret events in terms of what might happen; identify alternative courses of action and predict likely consequences of each; make a decision based on data obtained

Strategies: Double data discs, space bubble, paper dolls, Delphi technique, hypotheticals, consequences chart

Disciplines: Political science, law, sociology, science, language arts, art

Assessment: Practice portfolio

ONE

By the Book:
Learning History Beyond the Text

Social studies programs should include experiences that provide for the study of the ways human beings view themselves in and over time.

—NCSS Standard

Why I Use Historical Fiction in My Classroom

I use historical fiction as a hook to introduce an issue, illuminate a time period, and familiarize my students with lifestyles. Stories catch my students' interest and pique their curiosity; they are eager to research their predictions, confirm their ideas, and extend their understanding of themselves and their world by studying the past. By integrating literature, my students become participants in history rather than observers. Here's what Amy wrote at the end of our unit on westward expansion.

July 30, 1852
Dear Journal,
    This journey has been heart wrenching, thirst quenching, and most of all, an adventure I will never forget. We are settling in at this moment and by the time we arrived I knew this was the place to be. Astoria has pockets full of rich soil and a handful of opportunity.

Blending historical fiction with social studies brings history to life, increasing the likelihood that the historical journeys in my classroom will be ones my students never forget!

Historical Fiction Catches Kids' Attention

The first thing I do when I start a new unit in social studies is flood my classroom with all kinds of related books. It used to be mostly chapter books but lately I've been using picture books more often than not. In fact, one of the most vivid changes in my classroom is the presence of picture books. I can't imagine teaching without them. I get them from the public library, our school library, primary teachers, and my own collection. Some of them I read aloud to the kids. Some of them the kids read together. And some of them the kids read alone.

Historical fiction picture books are very user friendly. Even the least capable reader will find the pictures "readable." Yet picture books can stretch students, because the concepts in them are often more complex than those in the chapter books they can read independently. Children can make predictions, come up with generalizations, increase vocabulary, and discover new concepts while reading picture books. Picture books written about historical events generate excitement and invite questions. Issues become more visible. Patterns are established that students can replicate. Picture books are appropriate in intermediate and middle school classrooms!

Historically accurate picture books catch the kids' attention, creating an environment in which all kids can learn. They are the first step in building intellectual knowledge about a place, a period, or a group of people. History is hard for many children. They have no reservoir of analogies to draw from to help them out. Think about it: We are teaching children who cannot conceive of a time when all telephones were black and plugged into walls, when grocery stores sold only one kind of mustard, and when there were only three flavors of ice cream. How can we expect students to understand decisions made by people in the Revolutionary War period or the Mayan civilization without some appreciation for and knowledge of the way those decision makers lived?

I remind my students to look at the ways illustrations are used as we interpret information found in picture books. When possible, I find photographs to compare with the illustrations. We look for incongruities as well as confirmations. We try to discover what has been included and what has been left out.

Questions can arise from the story and the illustrations: "When I finish reading, I'd like you each to ask a question. The rule is, no question can be asked twice." Prior knowledge can be tapped: "Before reading the story, let's make a list of what you know about this topic." Investigations can be launched: "Now that we've looked at what happened to one pioneer family, let's do some research to see if their experience was typical or unusual."

It Provides a Common Classroom Experience

Some kids come to us with a wealth of background to draw on. Others have a meager fund of prior knowledge. It's important to balance these individual accounts as we begin any unit of study. By reading historical fiction, my students can more quickly conceptualize the past. The picture book format, particularly with its visual clues, helps my students construct meaning. Perhaps equally important, historical fiction gives my class a common understanding: When we move to group work, the groups have a shared experience from which to begin. Reading historical fiction aloud also promotes academic equity in my classroom. Finally, good historical fiction provides kids with an equal opportunity to develop historical analogies: "Isn't this like what we studied last month?"

It Bridges Past and Present

When kids relate to people in the past, the past doesn't seem so far away. Historical fiction acts as a bridge between the past and the present, making other times, other people, and other places seem alive. Picture books are especially powerful, providing both visual and contextual clues to how people lived, what their speech was like, and how they dressed, to their mind-set, their demeanor, and their manners. When accurately portrayed, these details are a savings account that students can draw on or supplement. Each deposit of information, whether a detail about social order, costume, creed, or attitude, swells the students' accounts, providing a richer understanding of the past and illuminating newly encountered knowledge. For example, in response to an assignment, *"Write a letter to Morning Girl. In the first paragraph, tell her something you learned from reading about her. In the second paragraph, tell her something you've learned from studying the historical period in which she lived. In the third paragraph, tell her how you feel about what happened to the Taino people"*, Alexa wrote:

Dear Imaginative Morning Girl,

Hi! You've taught me some interesting things. One of the truly great things you taught me is how important brothers and sisters are. The sentence, "Without him the silence is very loud" made me realize what a gift my brothers are. You taught me many other things too. But overall this is the most important.

Boy, did your lives change after contact with the explorers and other people who came. Didn't your lives change? From what I heard and learned, you got metal, tools, diseases, etc. The diseases really swept out your villages. I'm sorry!

I have mixed feelings about what happened. I really disagree with the idea of slavery. You aren't a people to be owned! You're a kind and gentle group in my opinion. But Europeans and other foreigners did give you useful things. You got cloth, mirrors, beads, and metal for tools. I wish those first explorers would have been nicer to you. You were kind to them and that proves you are a lovable people.

Yours always,
Alexa

P.S. You've made my imagination stretch!

It Presents People as Complex

Social studies texts are concerned primarily with breadth rather than depth. People, no matter how famous or important, are often reduced to a few sentences, and ordinary people seldom appear at all. Children have difficulty converting these often cryptic sketches into interesting, multifaceted individuals faced with hard choices. Consequently, myths abound and stereotypes flourish.

Good historical fiction presents people as they are, neither all good nor all bad, but somewhere in between. Kids can relate to characters in the story, identify with the universality of their behavior, and explore the outcome of their decisions. They may need a prompt: "Austin had to make a decision whether to stay in Oregon and claim his dad's property or go with his host family. Let's list the factors he had to consider before making his decision. Do you think Austin made a list? If not, how do you think he came to his decision? Would you have made the same decision?"

It Fills Out Issues

Most issues in life are multifaceted. If we were to depict an issue topographically there would be lumps and bumps, highs and lows, hills and valleys. Yet traditionally, historical issues have been presented to children as flat, unidimensional, single-sided. Historical fiction restores the landscape of history, helping kids see the past, "warts and all." They begin to comprehend that solutions are not always easy and dilemmas are common.

There are many ways to help bring this about; be creative. "Some men serving with the Patriots under General George Washington endured horrible conditions. Others ran away. Think about what you heard as I read *The Winter of Red Snow* aloud. Think about what you've read. Choose a buddy and together, write a newspaper editorial for a colonial paper discussing why people might act so differently."

It Personalizes Responses to Change and Challenge

When kids understand others, they also begin to know more about themselves and their heritage. Historical fiction puts people back into history. Children see how people, over time, have responded to challenges.

Often students can personalize these responses in contemporary ways: "Design a T-shirt for Abraham Lincoln during his early life.

Now, make a bumper sticker for Lincoln's life in New Salem. Next, create a yard sign representing Lincoln's political life in Springfield. Finally, make a billboard for Lincoln's life in the White House." Change can also be personalized: "Sarah Bishop went through several changes in the story. Make an illustrated time line of her life showing these changes. We don't know what happens to Sarah. Add a final marker to your time line, showing what you think happens to Sarah."

It Explores How Decisions Are Made

Historical fiction helps students explore how decisions are made. Some decisions are thoughtful; others are foolish. Some are logical; others are random. Some are individual; others are the result of consensus. Some follow a process; others are impromptu.

Historical fiction often provides an opportunity for kids to discuss

Featuring Historical Fiction

and debate the decisions. From the hindsight of history, my kids often make lists of the costs and benefits of decisions and then decide for themselves what would be best. My students like to create a living continuum to express their opinions about most any issue, whether historical or contemporary: "Pretend there is a line running from the back of our classroom to the front. The back of the line represents the opinion that the Patriots were 100 percent right in rebelling against King George and England, that wars like the Revolutionary War are justified. The front of the line represents the opinion that the Patriots didn't have to fight a war, that they could have worked out another way to get their freedom over time, that wars are never justified. When I signal, go stand where you are most comfortable. If you wish to stand in the middle, will you stand closer to the war-is-justifiable end of the line or with the war-is-never-justifiable end? Now, without talking, stand up for your opinion. In one minute, I'll be asking you to tell us why you are standing where you are. After we share our opinions, you'll have an opportunity to change your position if you'd like."

It Promotes Multiple Perspectives

Historical fiction helps children grow personally as well as academically. Having the students encounter characters who have different points of view or compare stories that present diverse perspectives develops an environment in which differences are appreciated. It is very important to me that my kids feel safe sharing their unique perspectives and that they respect the opinions of others.

Historical fiction includes many common examples of the different ways people deal with problems. It also acquaints students with the interpretive nature of history, showing how different authors and illustrators deal with the same issue.

Again, ways in which students can depict these perspectives can be nontraditional: "Let's create a point-of-view quilt showing how people during the Civil War felt. Think about the diverse views: Southerners, Northerners, free Blacks, enslaved Blacks, recent immigrants, pioneers. Choose three points of view and create a quilt square for each. Let's choose a background color for each group so we can easily sort them by point of view when we put our quilt pieces together."

It Connects Social Studies to the Rest of the Day

Historical fiction, while enhancing understanding of the past, can also be used to integrate social studies across the curriculum. For example, using a single book, *Dear Levi: Letters from the Overland Trail* by Elvira Woodruff, teachers can tap into activities in almost any discipline:

- *Language Arts:* You've already made it to Oregon. Write a letter to Austin offering him specific advice and encouragement.
- *Reading:* As you read pioneer books over the next two weeks, make journal entries about how you would feel in the main characters' shoes.
- *Math:* Conduct a five-question survey to see what at least fifteen fifth-graders know about wagon trains. Analyze your data and write a conclusion.
- *Geography:* Sketch three landmarks Austin might see on his journey on the Overland Trail.
- *Health:* Using the computer, research one disease or condition that pioneers frequently suffered from.
- *Art:* Design a button you would give Reuben to sew on his special "button coat."
- *Music:* Create a new verse for "Oh Susannah!" that reflects Austin's experiences.
- *Critical thinking:* Identify a problem Austin faced. With a partner, brainstorm at least three alternative solutions. Circle the one you like best and tell why.
- *Physical education:* Learn a square dance.

How I Help Students Discover Where the Story Stops and History Begins

It's easy to tell the difference between fact and fantasy in a Disney movie . . . the animals break into song. It's less obvious in the classroom. Where does the story stop and history begin? Using historical fiction in the classroom presents a challenge. How do we help our students differentiate between historical fiction and history? More fundamental, how can we help our students recognize the interpretative nature of historical reporting?

We Talk About It

I begin to raise my students' level of awareness by reviewing different genres of literature, two of which are historical fiction and history. I don't spend a lot of time identifying the differences early in the year, but I do plant the seeds by which my kids will be able to recognize them by reading two picture books back-to-back, one nonfiction, the other historical fiction. We compare, looking for similarities and differences. The differences often include voice (history is usually written in the third person while historical fiction is often in the first person), cast of characters (history is usually centered on "real, well-known people" while historical fiction often recounts the lives of "ordinary people"), and references (history tends to have a larger bibliography than historical fiction).

We Integrate Reading Skills

I ask my students to apply traditional reading skills such as distinguishing between fact and opinion, matching reading speed to purpose, and finding the main idea across the disciplines. This strengthens and deepens their learning across disciplines.

The contrast is often most stark when we compare a passage in the social studies text to historical fiction about the same topic. One of my favorite examples is the story of John Brown and the event at Harpers Ferry. Our social studies text devotes about twenty-three rather unrevealing words to him and it! *John Brown*, written by Gwen Everett and illustrated with Jacob Lawrence's vivid paintings, is told in the voice of John Brown's adolescent daughter. After we read this book together, my students have a clearer understanding not just of the man, but of the issues that drove him to the decisions he made. And they make the connections. Katrina, in writing about Lincoln, recalled that it was the

Kansas-Nebraska Act and John Brown's actions that caused Lincoln to reenter politics again:

> Lincoln was furious about the Kansas-Nebraska Act. That was an act that let the settlers of the Kansas and Nebraska Territories choose if they want to be a slave or a free state. Abe did not want to encourage or promote slavery, but of course things didn't go his way. Do not get me wrong, he was definitely not an abolitionist like John Brown, but he did not want to reinforce slavery.

We Encourage Questions

We need to develop a classroom environment in which questions are honored and teachers don't have to know all the answers. Many of us are not history experts, geography gurus, or wizards about the economy. Too often we stick with the questions in the social studies textbook because the answers are provided and we presume they are correct. Social studies then becomes an exercise in trying to guess what the textbook author is thinking. No wonder it's boring. Neither the teacher nor the kids have any ownership in what's happening. We need to encourage our students to ask genuine questions, not ones that have the answer printed in the teacher's edition. "Let's find out" are the three most invitational words in a teacher's vocabulary.

We Investigate Resources

When I read a book aloud to the class, I model how to look at the sources of information used by the author and the illustrator. The skill of evaluating resources becomes even more critical when students use the Internet to find information.

I provide students with more and more opportunities to evaluate who the information on the Internet is coming from. Kids need to understand that just because someone says it on the Net doesn't make it true. Having students check whether resources are cited, look at the author to see his/her credentials, and find documentation is as important as finding an answer to a question. Building healthy skepticism in ten-year-olds is an indicator of how education is changing as we begin a new century.

We Bring in Primary Documents

I frequently present primary documents in class so that we can analyze their reliability. We discuss possible biases and whether they reveal inaccuracies in the historical record. I help students recognize the difference between primary documents (a firsthand account); secondary accounts, also known as history (a historian's interpretation of past experience); and historical fiction (an author's personalization—the historian's interpretation with a dash of drama or humor).

We Download Documents Directly

The Internet has opened to my classroom a whole new resource, especially when it comes to primary documents. Recently, we were studying the Civil War and taking an in-depth look at Lincoln as a man and as a leader of men. As part of our study we read the picture book *The Gettysburg Address*, which is beautifully illustrated by Michael McCurdy. To provide the setting, I read Patricia Lee Gauch's short but powerful description of the Battle of Gettysburg, *Thunder at Gettysburg*, written from the eyewitness account of young Tillie Pierce. Then one of my students walked over to our classroom computer, went to Net Search on Netscape, typed in "The Gettysburg Address," and two drafts of the Gettysburg Address appeared in Lincoln's own handwriting! Additional typescripts showed all the changes between the drafts and the final copy. Not only could my students speculate about Lincoln's thoughts and motives, they could see the physical evidence of process writing from nearly 150 years ago! (For a more precise cyberspace address, try http://lcweb.loc.gov/exhibits/G.Address/gadrft.html Other multimedia historical collections from the Library of Congress National Digital Library currently available online can be found at http://www.loc.gov).

We Develop Social Studies Skills

When reading is integrated with social studies, it is critical that students read more than one book on a topic, that they are exposed to more than one kind of resource, and that they have an opportunity to discover multiple perspectives. Four separate but connected skills need to be learned, applied, and extended (NCSS Standards, 8):

- *Acquire information and manipulate data.* Students should be able to read, study, and search for information using social science methods and vocabulary as well as computers and other electronic media.
- *Develop and present policies, arguments, and stories.* Students should be able to classify, interpret, analyze, summarize, evaluate, and present information in well-reasoned ways that support better decision making for both individuals and society.
- *Construct new knowledge.* By way of valid social studies research, students should be able to increase their ability to conceptualize unfamiliar categories of information, establish cause/effect relationships, determine the validity of information/arguments, and develop new stories, models, narratives, pictures, or charts that add to their understanding of an event, idea, or person.
- *Participate in groups.* Students should be able to express and advocate reasoned personal convictions, recognize mutual ethical responsibility, negotiate conflicts and differences or maintain an individual position because of its ethical basis, and accept and fulfill the responsibilities associated with citizenship in a democratic republic.

We Establish Criteria

My students develop criteria for evaluating informational books and historical fiction. Elementary students are quite capable of identifying and comparing the specific characteristics of biographies, history, and historical fiction. For example, events in biographies or history books are predetermined, but made-up events can be inserted into historical fiction. Using a matrix that includes the characteristics of primary documents, history, biographies, and historical fiction, my students sift the similarities and differences until they can assign a category to each book they read.

We Bring in Resource People

My students and I invite experts into our classroom with whom we discuss observations, investigate questions, and explore point of view. An expert can be a grandmother who was interned during World War II, an uncle who has traveled extensively, or a local lawyer who can tell us how trials really work. I think it is important for my students to feel comfortable extending the invitation. Usually, a group of kids writes an invitation specifying the topic, the time frame of our study, and the length of the presentation. (Thirty minutes is long enough for most folks who aren't professional presenters.) The invitation also mentions those days and times that are best for our schedule. These same kids then deliver the invitation. The invited guest usually calls me to confirm that he or she will come, and when. After the presentations, another group of students writes thank-you notes.

We Test Generalizations

I am always alert for the inaccurate assumptions my students may make, such as "Kids in the past had it easier than we do today." I've learned to give them a litmus test for generalizations: Is this statement absolutely always true, absolutely always false, or some place in between? What evidence do you have?

Helping students look for errors, biases, and misinterpretations is one of the major roles we play as teachers. This kind of intellectual detective work is not only appropriate but essential to the continued growth and development of our students' understanding of history and acquisition of knowledge.

We Use Graphic Organizers

I help students analyze assumptions, scrutinize facts, and discern patterns by suggesting the use of graphic organizers. Diagrams, charts, and graphs help many students assimilate information from diverse resources and encourage critical thinking. As a bonus, graphic organizers help students stay on task so that discipline is more easily maintained. When I say, "Create a list," many kids just don't get immersed in the assignment. No surprise. However, those same kids will often engage with the subject matter if I suggest a graphic organizer for them to use. The example below demonstrates a pair share and discover organizer that only takes a piece of notebook paper folded lengthwise. Kids were buddy reading the first couple of chapters of *The Boys' War* by Jim Murphy. On one side of the paper, John wrote what he knew prior to reading. On the other side, Julian jotted down what he knew. In the middle of the paper, they listed new facts discovered during reading.

Facts John Already Knew

Boys could enlist pretty easy.

Sometimes they didn't have uniforms.

Facts Julian Already Knew

Boys were often drummers or buglers.

Facts That Are New to Both of Us

Many boys joined the army because they were bored of staying on the farm.

No way to check how old boys really were. (no computers!)

Sometimes their parents didn't know their sons were joining.

Volunteers for Confederates had to provide their own uniforms.

Sometimes people stole clothing from corpses to get a uniform.

Strategy for Success: The Walking in Their Shoes Interview

After we've read and discussed a biography of a historical person, I have my students pretend to be reporters interviewing that person. It's another way to link reading, language arts, and social studies. The kids begin by brainstorming questions a reporter might ask. They quickly dismiss questions that can be answered with a simple yes or no in favor of those requiring longer, more thoughtful answers. From the list of possible questions, each of the kids chooses six to ask in a

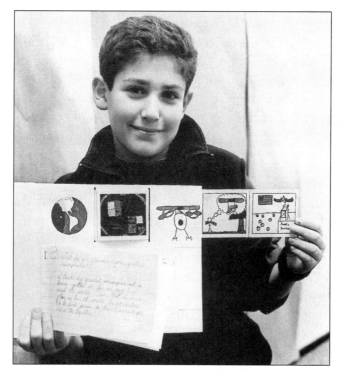

Sharing My Amelia Earhart Video Book and Interview

mock interview. Then they pretend to be the historical person and respond to all six questions in writing. This gives evidence of their reading comprehension and practice in writing. Voice, use of the present tense, and fluency are important language arts skills critical to the success of this strategy. Equally valuable social studies skills include sequencing, recognizing the significance of events, and demonstrating an appreciation for perspective.

Add visuals and kids who aren't strong writers can still complete this strategy with more success that just a writing assignment would allow. For each question, my kids draw a picture, creating a video book. The following is a sample from Kelly's video book which she made after reading a biography about Amelia Earhart, using the interview/picture strategy. (The video book strategy comes from a useful teacher resource, *Read! Write! Publish!* [Fairfax and Garcia 1992])

Interviewer: What do you do when you're not flying?

Amelia: I help work at the women pilots' organization, Ninety-nine. I also got involved in Zonta International. Zonta International is an organization for professional women in both professional and personal hobbies. I was also the first woman board member of any commercial airlines. I got some writing jobs.

Interviewer: What has been the hardest problem for you to overcome?

Amelia: People thought that I couldn't fly across the Atlantic Ocean because I was a woman. Why they thought this, I don't know, but inside I know we are all equals. I showed them when I made it across the Atlantic Ocean. I'm very proud of myself.

Whether illustrating cause and effect, recapping an event, or retelling history, this strategy is a useful way to analyze new knowledge, summarize a unit of study, and connect with other disciplines.

How I Plan a Cooperative Unit

We often do a cooperative westward expansion unit in the spring when the kids are developmentally ready for increased group indepen-

FIG. 1-1: *Kelly's Drawing Accompanies Her Amelia Earhart Interview*

dence. This cooperative unit provides many opportunities for students to solve problems (both academic and social), build self-confidence, and practice independent thinking.

Whenever I plan a unit, I first brainstorm ways my students can acquire knowledge, manipulate data, practice skills, and apply their understanding through group activities. Sometimes I do this with other teachers who are planning to teach the same basic content. Sometimes I do it by myself. I appropriate ideas I've heard other teachers share at conventions, ones I've read about in professional magazines, or ones I've picked up from Teachers Helping Teachers (http://www.pacificnet.net /~mandel) or Teacher's Edition Online (http://www.teachnet.com) on the Internet.

The following unit is based on several discussions I had with Oralee Kramer and Rick Moulden, from Chinook Middle School in Bellevue, Washington, who have been teaching a westward expansion unit with their eighth graders for the past several years. Using many of their ideas, I reshaped the unit to fit fourth and fifth graders, and to reflect my goals and objectives.

I Organize the Project in Pieces

I've found over the years that if I make the "bites" small enough, every child can succeed. I break down what my students need to do into small pieces. Due dates are critical. If the kids know when each piece of the project is due as well as what is expected, they're more likely to stay on course and less likely to be overwhelmed. Very few of us are naturally gifted long-term planners! Sequential due dates provide a model for attaining goals successfully. Additionally, informing students how much each part of the project is worth pays off. The students learn where to place their efforts and what they can knock off if they have to. Life is like that, and I want my classroom to be like life. Here's one example:

Moving Out—A Cooperative Project for Westward Expansion
Name:
Group Members:

Who is a pioneer? Many dictionaries say a pioneer is one who ventures into unknown or unclaimed territory to settle. You are going to have the exciting adventure of becoming pioneers and the opportunity to tell your story. You will be working in cooperative groups. Your group will become a family or a group of friends moving west or coming from Asia to settle in the Northwest. Together you will create a story about your trip based on historical fact.

1. You will need to read books and consult other related resources to make sure your trip is authentic. Keep track of the books your group read on the back of this paper.

   Points: 10 points for each book read

                   100 minimum points required per group member

   Date Due: 3/24

   Score:

Let's Begin the Trip West!

2. You will prepare a poster depicting all the members of your pioneer group. You will draw figures of each and clothe them appropriately. You will include a short biographical sketch for each.

   Points: 50 points maximum for figures in authentic dress
                  50 points maximum for descriptive paragraphs
   Due date: 3/27
   Score:

3. You will create a model of the wagon, ship, coach, or train that your group used to get to their new home. Each of the pioneers in your group must pack a small trunk of personal things he or she wants to take to the new home. Use the book *Grandma's Jewelry Box*, by Linda Milstein, as your model. You may find Joan Irvine's *How to Make Pop-ups* and *How to Make Super Pop-ups* especially helpful. You should also make a list of the things that you are bringing with you as a group.

   Points: 50 maximum for the model
                  50 maximum for the personal trunks
                  50 maximum for the list of shared items
   Due date: 3/31
   Score:

4. Your group will write a journal of at least ten entries to describe your trip. These entries should tell us many details about your journey. You should prepare sketches on overhead transparencies or on large construction paper that illustrate the scenes as you read the journal orally to the class. A map of your travel should accompany the journal.

   Points: 50 maximum for journal entries
                  50 maximum for sketches
                  50 maximum for the map
   Due date: 4/7
   Score:

5. Your group will suddenly fast-forward to today. Using a graphic organizer, compare the trip you've re-created with what the

trip would be like for your group today. You might want to use the diagrams from Parks and Black's *Organizing Thinking* (1990) or you may want to create your own. Compare and contrast at least five aspects of the trip (for example, length of time, safety, convenience, opportunities to discover things about yourself, and degree of group cooperation needed).

Points: 50 maximum for graphic organizer
Due date: 4/7
Score:

6. Your group will present the whole project to the class. You will have a maximum of fifteen minutes in which to do so. Please time and rehearse your presentation so you don't go over the time limit. All of the group members must participate in the presentation.

Points: 500 maximum for group presentation
Due date: 4/10
Score:

7. You will participate in three group conferences with your teacher during the project. You will cooperatively plan and work together to accomplish your goals. Evidence of such co-operation will be provided by you to the teacher. (Bring all planning sheets with you for each conference. You must turn these in during the final conference to receive credit for your work.)

First conference: Planning and goal setting
Due date: 3/25
Score:

Second conference: Mending and tending
Due date: 4/2
Score:

Third conference: Evaluation and recommendations
Due date: 4/8
Score:

Points: 100 maximum for evidence of:

a) efforts to solve problems peacefully
b) creation of a comfortable environment for all
c) collaboration on ideas so everyone feels included
d) contribution of a similar amount of work by each member

I Facilitate Knowledge

Kids need information before they begin any kind of a simulation. That's where I think most simulation activities fail. We often ask kids to manipulate history before they know any. Here's where historical fiction linked with factual accounts really pays off. In this unit, I require every student to read at least ten books before they can begin their journey west. We think of it as the ticket needed to begin. My students have to pack content about the westward trek just as the early pioneers packed their wagons with essentials for the journey. Most of the books are picture books or short histories, and they provide both a common understanding among group members and an opportunity for each student to contribute individually to the mutual effort needed to complete the journey successfully.

Provide Planning Sheets

Planning sheets are a big help to my students, who often have trouble beginning a cooperative activity because they can't decide what to do first. Planning sheets like the one that follows are organizational blueprints. They save time and increase productivity. Kids who are busy generally stay out of trouble, and that makes the classroom a nicer place for everyone. Additionally, research tells us that advance organizers increase student achievement (Educational Research Service, 13). Letting our students know what we think is important helps them focus on key ideas.

Planning the Journey

In your groups, discuss the following. You might want to take notes.

Starting point for the journey:

Destination:

Listen and Watch as We Read Our Pioneer Journal

Family or group members:

    Names:

    Ages:

    Why they want to move west:

    What they contribute to the journey:

Mode of travel:

Possible personal items:

Necessities that will be shared by the group:

Hardships on journey (description and result):

Good times on journey:

Landmarks and places visited:

Identify who will take major responsibility for each task:

Poster with descriptions of each person:

Model:

Trunks:

List:

Journals:

Maps:

Sketches:

Graphic Organizer:

We Share Products and Knowledge

After the kids have re-created the journey, it's important for them to share the work they've done and the things they've learned. I ask each group to present their trip to the whole class. It's fun and informative. The kids see other models, hear other ideas, and store away new strategies that they can use during later units. Making a presentation also calls into play the communication skills that need to be continually practiced in our classrooms.

We Assess the Project

Since this is a cooperative project, an individual assessment from each group member about how it went is natural and authentic. Self-reflection followed by a group reflection promotes positive learning. Helping students become aware of traits and behavior that either help or hinder group processes is time-consuming and requires sensitivity and trust but is well worth the investment. Remember, this unit often occurs after the students have been sharing the same classroom and teacher for six months. I wouldn't do an assessment like this the first month of school.

Group Assessment

Name:

Directions: Each individual in the group answers on paper independently and brings answers to final conference.

Let's Make a Play Out of Our Presentation

1. How would you rate your contribution to the group?   – ✓ +
   Explain:
2. How would you rate the cooperation of the group?   – ✓ +
   Explain:
3. What went well?
4. What would you do differently next time?

We Keep the Focus

Sometimes students' attention begins to wander during presentations by their classmates. I use response sheets to help the kids stay focused and to provide feedback to each group that presents. I also use these response sheets to stimulate reflection during small-group evaluations.

Response Sheet for Student Listeners: Westward Expansion
When you are not presenting, you are expected to be an attentive learning audience. This sheet will help direct your listening and thinking skills.

1. Were members of the group introduced and described?
2. Do you know what necessities the group packed?
3. Did they describe a hardship they faced on their journey?

We've Done It! We Made It to Oregon!

4. Was there an event or happening during the journey that made them happy?
5. Did their journal entries seem realistic? thoughtful? complete?
6. Did the sketches support the journal entries?
7. Could you see evidence of group cooperation?
8. Overall rating on group presentation:

smattering of applause

round of applause

standing ovation

Endnote

Dear Kara, Caitlyn, Evan, and Andrew,

I just wanted to write you a note to let you know my response to your Westward Expansion project and presentation.

First of all, let's talk about your products.

Your people poster was excellent. I especially liked the care you took to craft your people and the interesting biographies you made to accompany them. You are the first group ever to have twins go west. Good thinking.

Your map was accurate and easy to read. I enjoyed following your trail and appreciated how you located each important stop and landmark along the way.

Your trunks are wonderful. I loved the way you took so much care to present each of the characters with their own special items that reflected their individual personality. The three-dimensional trunk was unique. I liked the way your trunk was organized.

Second, let's take a look at your wagon:

Wow! Your wagon was the prototype for all that came later. You set the standard with your incredibly detailed and accurate model. I am so impressed with the time and care you took to create such a fabulous replica. I also appreciated the "inside look" that accompanied your wagon. I know the cooperation and out-of-school time it took. You really exceeded the assignment, "above and beyond." Doesn't that feel good? I love it.

Third, your presentation:

Well done! I loved the costuming, the background, and the props. You did a fine job of mixing creativity and knowledge as you led us west through your excellent journal entries. I liked the way you shared the tasks, just like a pioneer family would have done over one hundred years ago!

Finally, your group work:

I want to congratulate you all on working through the rough times when you didn't all agree. You continued to see strengths in each other, even when you had different ideas. You continued to appreciate what each person brought to the group and those gifts were reflected in your entire presentation. Working in a group isn't ever easy but it often is rewarding. I hope you feel like this was a rewarding experience. You certainly made it wonderful for those of us watching. Thank you.

Sincerely yours,
Mrs. L.

Bibliography for Westward Expansion

A good selection of resources, at varying reading levels, makes all the difference in how well and how much my students learn from a unit such as the one I've just described. I've used the list below in my classroom with great success. (This list is a beginning; it grows and improves each time I teach the unit.)

BEATTY, PATRICIA. 1993. *Bonanza Girl*. New York: William Morrow. Chapter book about a family that leaves Portland, Oregon, for the gold fields of the Idaho Territory in the 1880s. Lively and readable.

CONRAD, PAM. 1991. *Prairie Visions: The Life and Times of Solomon Butcher*. New York: HarperCollins. Wonderful photos and easy text about the life of the "soddies" in early Nebraska.

COONEY, BARBARA. 1994. *Only Opal: The Diary of a Young Girl*. New York: Putnam. Based on the diary of a real person. Beautiful!

EMSDEN, KATHARINE. 1992. *Voices from the West: Life Along the Trail*. Carlisle, MA: Discovery Enterprises, Limited. Paperback collection of essays, poetry, and excerpts from diaries of three travelers in the mid-1800s presents a variety of perspectives relating to life along the trail west.

ERICKSON, PAUL. 1995. *Daily Life in a Covered Wagon.* New York: John Wiley & Sons. If I could have only one book to teach about westward expansion, I would choose this one. Engaging, accurate, and full of pictures, this book lets my students truly grasp what it means to "move west." Now out in paperback. Get a classroom set!

FISHER, LEONARD EVERETT. 1990. *The Oregon Trail.* New York: Holiday House. Authentic photographs, easy-to-read text, great map, and interesting quotes.

HARNESS, CHERYL. 1995. *The Amazing Impossible Erie Canal.* New York: Simon & Schuster. Charming picture book documentary of the building of the Erie Canal.

HARVEY, BRETT. 1988. *Cassie's Journey: Going West in the 1860's.* New York: Holiday House. Based on actual accounts. Engaging picture book.

———. 1993. *My Prairie Year.* New York: Holiday House. Based on the diary of Elenore Plaisted. Wonderful picture book.

KNIGHT, AMELIA STEWART. *The Way West: Journal of a Pioneer Woman.* Outstanding pictures combined with authentic journal of a family's move to the Oregon Territory in 1853.

KUDLINSKI, KATHLEEN V. 1996. *Facing West: A Story of the Oregon Trail.* New York: Viking. Easy-to-read chapter book that chronicles a family's journey from Missouri to Oregon in 1845. Good for all the students to read or to be read aloud.

LEVINE, ELLEN. 1992. . . . *If You Traveled West in a Covered Wagon.* New York: Scholastic. Good basic facts for all the students.

MILSTEIN, LINDA. 1992. *Grandma's Jewelry Box.* New York: Random House. Pattern book to show the students how they might "pack a paper trunk" for the way west in three dimensions!

MURPHY, DAN. 1992. *Oregon Trail, Voyage of Discovery: The Story Behind the Scenery.* Las Vegas: K.C. Publications. Written by a park ranger, this is an excellent source to read aloud to give all the children access to basic information.

NIXON, JOAN LOWERY. 1988. *A Family Apart.* New York: Bantam.

———. 1989. *Caught in the Act.* New York: Bantam.

———. 1989. *In the Face of Danger.* New York: Bantam.

———. 1996. *A Place to Belong.* New York: Bantam. Called the "orphan train quartet," these four books are based on facts about the 200,000 children brought west by the New York Home Society from 1830 to 1920. Although they are written sequentially, kids enjoy reading them in any order. I do recommend reading *A Family Apart* first, just to provide a more thorough picture of the setting for the other three books.

ROUNDS, GLEN. 1994. *The Prairie Schooners.* New York: Holiday House. Excellent paperback resource with easy-to-read text about the wagon trains to Oregon from 1843 to 1868. Highly recommended!

SANDERS, SCOTT RUSSELL. 1989. *Aurora Means Dawn.* New York: Simon & Schuster. Picture book about moving to Ohio in the early 1800s.

———. 1992. *Warm as Wool.* New York: Simon & Schuster. Super picture book that helps us all understand history. A book of hope and wisdom as well as information.

SANDLER, MARTIN W. 1994. *Pioneers.* New York: HarperCollins. A Library of Congress book with stunning photographs and a very accessible text for intermediate grades.

SAN SOUCI, ROBERT D., and BRIAN PINKNEY. 1993. *Cut from the Same Cloth: American Women of Myth, Legend, and Tall Tale.* New York: Putnam. Collection of wonderful tales about strong women of historical America.

SORENSON, HENRI. 1995. *New Hope.* New York: Lothrop, Lee & Shepard. A great "connector" book blending westward expansion with immigration.

TURNER, ANN. 1989. *Dakota Dugout.* New York: Simon & Schuster. Short picture book about prairie pioneers that provides models of several literary devices: atmosphere, flashback, imagery, metaphor, and simile.

———. 1997. *Grasshopper Summer.* New York: Simon & Schuster. Engaging chapter book about a young boy and his family who move from Kentucky to Dakota Territory.

VAN LEEUWEN, JEAN. 1992. *Going West.* New York: Dial. Picture book that recounts the challenges faced by a pioneer family during their first year in the West.

———. 1994. *Bound for Oregon.* New York: Dial. Wonderful chapter book based on a true account. Van Leeuwen became intrigued with the westward journey during her research for *Going West,* so she wrote this very authentic and interesting book. Telling about a family's move from Arkansas to Oregon in 1852, this book provides a rich understanding of the way west. Believable young girl as main character.

WOODRUFF, ELVIRA. 1994. *Dear Levi: Letters from the Overland Trail*. New York: Knopf. Great informative chapter book that manages to avoid the stereotypes often found in books about westward movement. Contact between Native Americans and pioneers is especially sensitive. Wonderful format for teaching friendly letters. Works great as a read-aloud. The main character is a young boy.

TWO

A Place at the Table: Investigating Global Issues in a Day

Social studies programs should include experiences that provide for the study of global connections and interdependence.
—NCSS Standard

Hunger. Homelessness. War. There's no end to the issues that are persistent, contemporary, and global. Most school curriculums ask us to concentrate on history and geography; few of us are expected to do more than recognize worldwide problems during weekly current-events activities. However, I think we not only can but must offer our students experiences that demonstrate the connectedness of issues around the globe, introduce ways of looking at such issues, and explore what can be done about them from different points of view.

Persistent Issues/Dilemmas

The National Council for the Social Studies (NCSS) identifies several persistent dilemmas that provide ample opportunities for exploring solutions reflecting two or more points of view. These dilemmas include:

individual beliefs/majority rule, obeying the law/right to dissent, cultural variety/cultural assimilation, community progress/individual liberties, individual rights/public safety, national security/

individual freedom, worker security/employee rights, free enterprise/public planning, global business competition/national interest, and national/state/local-community control (NCSS, 9–10)

Common and Multiple Perspectives

Helping students construct a blend of personal, academic, pluralist, and global views is the NCSS-recommended way to go.

We can help students construct a personal perspective by giving them opportunities to investigate issues and consider the implications to themselves and their families. They need to have a chance to explore costs and benefits, to identify responsibilities, and to discuss the consequences of their choices.

Students should also be helped to construct an academic perspective by looking at an issue from specific points of view. The informed social studies teacher promotes this kind of learning by introducing students to multiple ways of looking at an issue and analyzing more than one solution.

A pluralist perspective finds its way into our students' repertoire as they experience respect for differences of opinion and preference in the classroom. Our students need to learn that these differences are not problems but healthy attributes of a democratic society.

Finally, our students need to construct a global perspective. They need to be encouraged to view the world and its people with understanding and concern. They need to develop a sense of responsibility and a commitment to finding peaceful and fair solutions to world problems.

World Day of Hunger

Nowhere in my curriculum, social studies or otherwise, am I required to teach about hunger. In fact, there's not even an option to teach about it. But teach about it I do.

Maybe I'm a little nuts. First, why teach something I don't have to? There's not enough time to do what I'm required to do. Second, my students are young. They have enough to worry about without taking on world problems. Finally, there are no materials, texts, or guidelines provided, so what do I teach?

Why Teach Something I Don't Have To?

I teach it because I care. I teach it because I want my students to care. I teach it because it's part of helping students learn to connect knowledge, skills, and values to active citizenship, whether local or global. Fitting new information, experiences, and feelings into existing knowledge enriches and extends what students know. The practice of acquiring, manipulating, classifying, interpreting, analyzing, summarizing, and evaluating information enhances what students can do. Helping my kids weigh priorities when values conflict encourages them to examine their own feelings and beliefs.

Why Should My Kids Learn About a Depressing Thing Like Hunger?

Students who possess knowledge, skills, and values are ready to take appropriate civic action. What is appropriate for a fourth grader may be very different from what is appropriate for an eighth grader, but both are ready to do *something*. Social studies that culminates in a paper-and-pencil test of facts is shallow. Social studies that concentrates on creating time lines or completing a chapter outline lacks meaning.

Supporting the common good is critical to the full development of a citizen in a democracy. The development of "student-citizens," young people who will soon assume the role of citizen, is the purpose of social studies education. Young people need to understand the complexity of the world they will inherit; they need to manipulate ideas, respect and support the dignity of the individual, and care about the common good of the local and global community.

So What Do I Teach?

Woven through all the subjects my students and I regularly study in a day are three kinds of experiences: head, hands, and heart.

The head experiences center on knowledge. Old knowledge is shared: *What do you know about hunger? Have you ever been really hungry? Who's hungry in our community? the state? the nation? the world? Write a definition for hunger.* New knowledge is discovered, disseminated, and documented. Over the years I have collected resources to help the students understand the causes and results of hunger. Most of these resources are free, and they are listed at the end of this chapter.

The hands experiences focus on doing—manipulating information through the multiple intelligences. Writing, reading, categorizing, constructing, organizing, discussing, illustrating, singing, simulating, resolving, and reflecting contribute to developing well-reasoned ways of making decisions that benefit both individuals and society.

The heart experiences are critical. The road through an educational unit that stimulates compassion is full of potholes. Value-based social studies teaching and learning is powerful. I need to make sure that my students are aware of the complex dilemmas a particular issue comprises. I need to make sure my kids have an opportunity to evaluate each potential solution in terms of its costs and benefits to various groups. Additionally, I must be wary of injecting my own biases and opinions, must encourage my students to recognize opposing points of view, and must be sensitive to cultural similarities and differences.

As part of caring, my kids need to do something about the issue. This deflects the uncomfortable feelings of guilt children often experience when introduced to persistent issues and dilemmas. Action is an antidote to guilt. Informed, thoughtful action, whether by individuals or groups, is the beginning of a solution. A solution to even the most difficult global problem can begin in a classroom.

Planning

I like to let the parents of my students know what we are doing in the classroom, especially when I move from the regularly scheduled curriculum to a one-day concentration on a topic. Frequently, parents volunteer to share their special expertise or to support our activities in some way. For World Day of Hunger, I usually send home a letter in advance (see Appendix 2-1). Most years, I have my

World Day of Hunger on or near World Food Day (October 16). Some years I set aside a day between Thanksgiving and Winter Break.

Making Connections

We begin almost every day with math. World Day of Hunger is no exception. I greet each child with a smile and a four-by-six-inch index card, which becomes his or her good-humor graph—a line graph with the hours of the day (nine to four) as the horizontal axis and a good-humor continuum (zero is "grouchy" and ten is "on top of the world") as the vertical axis. Throughout the day, we take an hourly check on how we are feeling, and then we discuss the graph at the end of the day. Sometimes we use a circle, divided into hourly segments, and put happy faces, okay faces, or sad faces to record our feelings.

Including the Multiple Intelligences

Next we construct a wondershape. (The wonder of this strategy is that it took me so many years to think of it!) The wondershape began as a way to check reading comprehension that didn't rely on written questions and answers yet allowed the students to demonstrate their understanding.

I wanted to do this by including all the kids in my classroom in a common activity. After teaching the essential elements of a story, I asked my students to create a "wondershape" in which they detailed the story through pictures. I started with a circle because it is easy. All the kids needed was a template and one demonstration.

I then discovered that this strategy works incredibly well as an organizer or manager of information. And because this strategy is built on the mathematical concept of symmetry, it only takes a gentle nudge to encourage kids to explore other symmetrical shapes.

The wondershape strategy taps into a number of the intelligences. It appeals to the kinesthetic learner, since paper needs to be manipulated. The visual learner enjoys drawing pictures and creating

Hunger Balls Reflect Our Day

shapes, while linguistic intelligence is used to add the headings or descriptions. The logical-mathematical learner is engaged by the sequential organization of the strategy. Interpersonal intelligence is included if students are asked to share their wondershape. Intrapersonal reflection is encouraged by asking students to write thoughtfully about what they learned (head), what they did (hands), and how they felt (heart.)

When I begin using this strategy, I often specify the elements I want included, but by the end of the year my students choose what they will illustrate or how they will organize their wondershape. If they illustrate the four most important parts of a story, it is very easy for me to see who "got it" and who didn't. If they identify five Civil War issues, I can quickly assess their accuracy as well as their ability to organize information. If they accumulate facts about hunger, I can evaluate their ability to acquire information and manipulate data as well as gain some insight into what they value.

This strategy is also a way for kids to put stories back together. Sometimes I think we analyze stories too much, fragmenting them beyond recognition. Some of our students lose the sense of the story or focus only on the separate parts of an experience. They can't see the forest for the trees. Symmetrical shapes seem to help these literal learners see the whole and remind the others of where they've been and what they've done.

For World Day of Hunger, we use the wondershape strategy to organize information and record discoveries in a "hunger ball." The symmetrical shape reminds us how interrelated this global issue truly is. (See Appendix 2-2 for directions.)

Some years we make hunger booklets instead of hunger balls. These quickly folded eight-page "little" books are also effective organizers and help kids manage information effectively and efficiently. (See Appendix 2-3 for directions.)

Hour by Hour

My organizational structure for World Day of Hunger is straightforward and linear: we learn something about hunger every hour. My goal is to instill new information and thoughts about hunger while still maintaining my regular schedule as much as possible. I use a variety of materials and media (see the resources listed at the end of this chapter).

I usually make an overhead transparency of each piece of information and make photocopies of it to distribute to the kids. Each hour we discuss an overhead and then the kids cut and paste their copies into their hunger ball or hunger book. After our discussion, I ask the kids to write a set of "know, do, feel" sentences about what we focused on during that hour. "Know" means to identify something they've learned, "do" means to recount one thing they did or might do with this information, and "feel" requires an insight about or an appreciation of the information.

9:00   The Kids Are Eager for the Day to Begin

Know:

> Learn about hunger here and around the world.
>
> Discover what it has to do with us.
>
> Determine whether we can do anything about it.

Do:

> Begin creating a hunger ball or hunger book to organize information and record discoveries.
>
> Watch *Famine and Chronic Persistent Hunger: A Life and Death Distinction* video.

Feel:

> Record feelings on the good-humor graph. Note: *I see lots of smiles and happy graphs.*

10:00   The Groundwork's Been Laid:
Now We Need to Get Active

Know:

> Introduce the hunger cycle overhead from UNICEF.
>
> Discuss.

Do:

> Incorporate copy of the hunger cycle into the hunger ball or hunger book.

Exploring the Hunger Cycle

Feel:

Record feelings on the good-humor graph. Note: *Still lots of happy graphs and smiley faces.*

11:00   *Time to Build a Global Community*

Know:

Recognize that people all over the world share common words to communicate, such as *hello, friend, thank you,* and *good-bye.*

Do:

Play the Language Game (see Appendix 2-4) to introduce the kids to languages around the world.

Have representatives from each group write their greeting on the board and let everyone try to guess what language it is.

Add other languages students know.

Include several of the greetings in the hunger ball or hunger book.

Feel:

Comment on what this activity had to do with World Day of Hunger and reflect on what has been learned.

Record feelings on the good-humor graph. Note: *Oops. Some kids are starting to get hungry. The graphs are showing a definite decline.*

12:00 Noon

Know:

List and discuss hunger myths and facts.

Do:

Fill out the opinion poll (see Appendix 2-5).

Discuss the statements.

Let the children who wish to change their answers do so. (It's important not to determine a "right" answer but to stimulate thinking and provide a conducive atmosphere for discussing weighty issues in the classroom.)

Paste the completed opinion poll into the hunger ball or hunger book.

Feel:

Record feelings on the good-humor graph and write a reflection about this activity.

12:30   *Lunch—Rice Has Never Smelled So Good!*

The kids are starving—or at least they think they are! Spoon servings of rice into paper bowls. Give each student chopsticks and a paper cup of water. Offer soy sauce to those who wish. (Over the years I've learned to be the dispenser; too much soy sauce and the kids won't eat their rice. In my classroom, kids who swear they hate rice gobble up their serving and ask for more. Others eat more slowly, savoring each mouthful. Some sit and look at their chopsticks, mystified. After a quick chopstick lesson, some of them become more animated. Plastic forks to the rescue of those who still sit.

As the kids eat, have them discuss what to do with the lunch money they have donated. (Some possibilities: UNICEF is a United Nations agency that helps children around the world lead healthier, more comfortable lives. The Hunger Project is an organization dedicated to ending hunger in the world. Here in Washington State, Northwest Harvest is a local food bank.)

1:30

Know:

Become aware of the Declaration of the Rights of the Child.

Do:

Illustrate the ten principles of the Declaration (see Appendix 2-6).

Before starting this activity, I read Michael Rosen's *The Greatest Table: A Banquet to Fight Against Hunger*. In addition to being a perfect topic for this day, the book also provides a pattern for the class book we'll soon be creating about children's rights. Its accordion format is one children enjoy replicating. Its different styles of illustration, by sixteen favorite children's book artists, including Chris Van Allsburg, Patricia Polacco, and Anita Lobel, provide a variety of visual prompts for my kids as they construct their own books.

I divide my class into three groups of ten and each group creates a book. To cut down on "deciding time," I put the numbers one through ten in a hat, and the kids draw a number and then create a picture to match the principle with that number. I use drawing paper that has been cut nine inches by ten inches, and have the kids place a half-inch fold at each end of the longer width. This leaves a nine-by-nine-inch square drawing surface with folded edges on two sides. The two folded edges are treated as borders and are used to create the accordion effect.

2:30   Engaged! Engrossed!
The Class Is Ready for Our Simulation

Know:

Learn how the distribution of the world population compares with the world food supply eaten daily.

Putting an Accordion Book Together

Do:

Experience the following simulation. (Several curriculum resources listed in the bibliography include a variation of this activity. This one is adapted from *Children Hungering for Justice*. I thank Marj Montgomery and Deb Parks for their collaboration.)

1. Designate five geographic locations in the room: Asia and the Pacific, Africa, Latin America and the Caribbean, the United States and Canada, Europe and Russia.
2. Break the class into groups that reflect the distribution of the world population by region (see Figure 2-1). In a class of thirty, for example, seventeen would be designated Asia/Pacific; three Africa; three Latin America/Caribbean; two United States/ Canada; and five Europe/Russia.

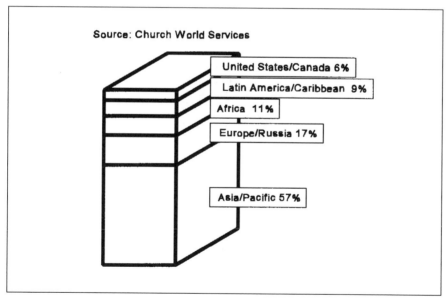

Source: Church World Services

United States/Canada 6%

Latin America/Caribbean 9%

Africa 11%

Europe/Russia 17%

Asia/Pacific 57%

FIG. 2-1: *Distribution of the World Population*

3. Now hand the groups something that represents the percentage of the world's daily food consumption by region (see Figure 2-2). (Raisins, M&M's, or hard candies are possible choices. My kids' favorite is little cracker goldfish. I used peanuts until I found out how many kids have severe peanut allergies. Non-food items such as baseball cards, coupons, or pennies can also be used.)

4. Ask the children in each group to share how they feel about their group and the other groups in terms of how many units each received. (The first thing I usually hear is *Hey, that's not fair.* It's pretty obvious that the treats have been unequally distributed.)

5. Explain that the world can be divided into two groups: developed countries, where about one quarter of the total people on earth live and can get the basics of food, clean water, and health care relatively easily; and developing countries, where over three quarters of the world's population live and have difficulty just surviving.

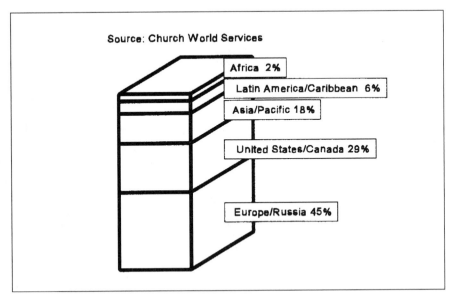

FIG. 2-2   *Share of the World Food Supply Eaten Daily*

6. Ask the kids to look around the room and decide whether they think the regions with a lot of food should share with those that have less.
7. Discuss this issue thoughtfully, listening to each student's point of view and proposing ways that the sharing might be accomplished. (It's not an easy task. The thing I avoid is making the kids feel guilty. Instead, we brainstorm how resources might be shared so that all children can get enough to eat.)

Feel:

Fill in the last page of the hunger book or the last segment of the hunger ball. (Have the kids write about what they have learned today, what they did, and how they feel. A number of comments from students in one of my classes follows.)

What Kids Have Said About World Day of Hunger

Hunger isn't just in Seattle, it's all over the world. We talked about things, we watched videos. We even had a lunch of only rice and water. I learned a lot about hunger. My favorite thing I did was separate into countries/continents and get the amount of riches each place had. We learned about greed and sharing among countries. UNICEF helps stop greed and war. I really liked learning about hunger!—Kendra

The earth produces enough food for all the people on earth, even the hungry people. We could go and help the hungry people start a life, help them get started. I feel that people aren't doing all they can to help hungry people. I also feel a little sorry for the hungry kids and adults.—Chelsea

For World Hunger Day we watched two films, made this book, and did an activity where we divided into groups and distributed marshmallows for food. We also skipped lunch and had rice and water. From the films I learned the difference between famine and chronic, persistent hunger. I know that 35,000 people die of hunger every single day. Twenty-four people die a minute. We can learn and understand about hunger and then we can react accordingly. I have mixed feelings. I feel sad, unhappy, angry, and scared. I also feel glad that I have food to eat.—Dana

Make a final entry on the good-humor graph. Note: *Happy faces, thoughtful faces, thankful faces are all around the room.*

Endnote

A one-day study is not comprehensive. It is more like window-shopping or wandering around the mall checking out the shops. The one-day study introduces various possibilities for later exploration, piques interest, and stimulates ideas and attitudes. A one-day study is usually teacher-instigated and carefully planned.

However, when you do a one-day study, you need to be prepared for what may follow. Suppose you do a World Day of Hunger. Now imagine that one of your kids discovers that the Universal Declaration of Human Rights was adopted by the United Nations in 1948, largely as a result of the efforts of Eleanor Roosevelt. In 1989, the United Nations General Assembly adopted the Declaration of the Rights of the Child. By 1997, 188 nations had ratified that declaration. Only Somalia, the United Arab Emirates, Oman, the Cook Islands, and the United States have not begun the ratification process. How would your kids react?

Most Americans have not even heard of the Declaration of the Rights of the Child. Those who favor the ratification believe it will improve the lives of American children, ensuring consistent government support for education and health as well as protection from exploitation and abuse. Those who oppose ratification do so for two main reasons: fear that it will undermine the family and fear that it will weaken U.S. sovereignty.

In my classroom, this information gave our study a new focus. My class decided to simulate a mock UN debate, write letters expressing their point of view to people in positions of power, and set up a survey to see how the people in our community felt about the issue.

The one-day study frequently becomes a springboard for further exploration that is student-directed rather than teacher-led and often culminates in social action or community service. My kids have collected money for the hungry, sponsored clothing drives for the homeless, written letters to legislators suggesting solutions for hunger, created school supply packs for students in developing countries, and purchased seed and animals for farming projects overseas. This kind of exploration is personal to individual classrooms and empowers kids enormously; it is the essence of participatory citizenship. And it begins with bringing global issues into the classroom. I know that my students become more informed and connected to the wider community because of experiences like World Day of Hunger. What they *do* ignites a concern for the welfare of our planet. How they *feel* transcends simple acts of charity, providing a lifelong model for problem solving.

Appendix 2-1:
Letter to Parents Regarding World Day of Hunger

Dear Parent(s),

As the children gear up for Halloween and Thanksgiving, we'd like to shift gears and take a day to investigate world hunger. We think that fifth graders are compassionate and caring young people who can make a difference. We have observed that learning about the causes and effects of hunger stimulates thoughtful responses as these young people become more aware of global issues.

Our World Day of Hunger will take place on [date]. We urge the children to eat a hearty breakfast and to leave their lunches at home. Throughout the day, the children will be learning about hunger—its causes and effects and what can be done about it. For lunch, we will stay in our classrooms and eat a bowl of rice and drink water. Children who wish to may donate the cost of their usual lunch to an organization that works to reduce hunger, such as Northwest Harvest, UNICEF, or the Hunger Project.

We anticipate this day-long integrated focus on hunger will stimulate discussion at the family dinner table that night. Your children will share with you their information, insights, and reflection.

Thank you for your support.

Sincerely yours,

The Fifth-Grade Teachers

P.S. We need three or four electric rice cookers for each class. If you have one you could loan us, please send it to school that day with your child. Please label lid, cord, and pot. Thanks very much.

Appendix 2-2: Wondershape

This is an activity that promotes problem-solving, explores symmetry, offers open-ended choices, and contributes to personal connections. After the students have decided on the number of categories (such as parts of speech), classification (such as invertebrates), steps (such as the water cycle), or issues (such as the five issues that contributed to the Civil War), they should do the following:

1. Using drawing paper, cut four or more identical symmetrical shapes about six inches or more in diameter. Put one step or category on each shape. Use words and pictures.
2. Fold each shape in half, keeping the drawing/words inside.
3. Put glue on one half of the outside of the shape and attach it to one half of the outside of the second shape.
4. Glue the other half of that shape to one half of the outside of a third shape, and so on until all the shapes are connected.
5. Tie a length of string to a paper clip and attach to the wondershape. Suspend from the ceiling.

Many teachers use this for practicing facts, for example, multiplication spheres or division spheres. Others use it to illustrate life cycles

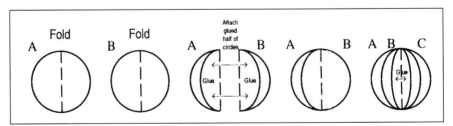

FIG. 2-3: *Wondershape Diagram*

or to classify characteristics of plants or animals. Some use it to retell the important parts of a story or demonstrate understanding of a historical event. It's also a good organizer for a series of activities related to a topic, such as World Hunger Day.

Appendix 2-3: Directions for "Little" Book

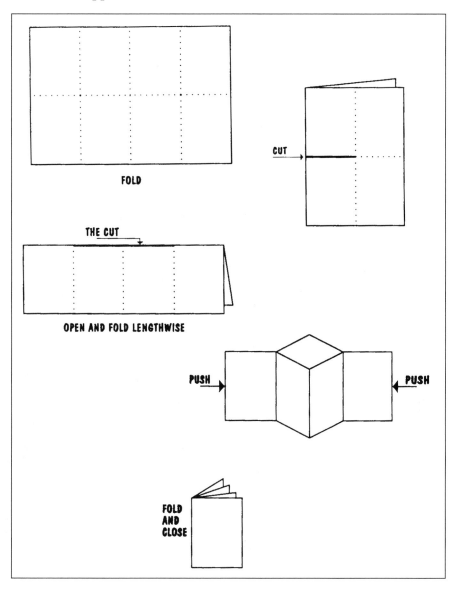

Appendix 2-4: The Language Game

The Language Game was developed by REACH, a multicultural educational corporation in the Seattle area that pioneered infusing multicultural and global education into the regular classrom curriculum.

On index cards, one for each child, write—regularly and phonetically—the word for a common expression or term in a foreign language. (I like to use *hello* or *friend*, since all languages have greeting words and a word for *friend*.) Write the word in a number of languages, dividing the number of kids in the class by the number of languages being used to determine how many times to use each one; that way, each language will be fairly equally represented. (I make it a point to use languages spoken by children in the class, or by their parents or ancestors.) There is a list at the end of this appendix to get you started.

Hand each child a card: "Please keep your word secret right now. When I signal, start saying your word loud enough for others to hear. Move around the room and find others who are saying the same word. When you find another person who is saying your word, become a group and listen for others who are saying your word. When you think you have found everyone who has the same word, gather in a corner of the room and keep saying your word until I give the signal to stop."

After all the groups have formed, have the kids guess what language they were speaking and what the word meant.

Spanish

Hello	Hóla (oh-la)
Friend	Amigo (ah-mee-goh)
Thank you	Gracias (grah-see-ahs)
Good-bye	Adiós (ah-dee-ohs)

Chinese

Hello	Nei ho mah (nay-hoh-mah)
Friend	Pong yew (pong-you)

Thank you Daw jeah (daw-jeah)
Good-bye Joi geen (joy-geen)

Korean

Hello Yobosaeyo (yoh-boh-say-yoh)
Friend Chinku (chin-koo)
Thank you Komapseupnida (ko-map-soop-nei-da)
Good-bye Anyonghikeishipsheyo (ahn-young-hee-kei-ship-shi-yoh)

Pilipino Tagalog

Hello Kumista (koo-moos-tah)
Friend Kaibigan (kah-e-bee-gan)
Thank you Salamat (sah-lah-mat)
Good-bye Paalam (pah-ah-lam)

Lakota (Native American)

Hello Hau (how)
Friend
    Male Kola (koh-lah)
    Female Kicuwa (kee-soo-wa)
Thank you Pila (pee-lah)
Good-bye Ahke (ah-ken)

Vietnamese

Hello
    Mr. Chao Ong (chow um)
    Mrs. Chao Ba (chow bah)
    Miss Chao Co (chow koh)
Friend Ban (bahn)
Thank you Cam on (kahm-ong)
Good-bye Same as *hello*

Appendix 2-5: Hunger Opinion Poll

Name_____

Write A for Agree, D for Disagree, or N for Don't Know

_____ 1. There's simply not enough food.

_____ 2. Nature is to blame; sometimes there's enough and sometimes there's not.

_____ 3. There are just too many mouths to feed.

_____ 4. We can't have enough food and protect the environment.

_____ 5. Boosting food production through scientific advances is the answer.

_____ 6. If land was redistributed more fairly, food production would drop.

_____ 7. If governments would get out of the way, business could stop hunger.

_____ 8. There have always been poor and hungry people.

_____ 9. The United States should increase foreign aid to end hunger.

_____10. Hunger isn't America's problem.

Appendix 2-6: The Ten Principles of the Declaration of the Rights of a Child (*Source:* A Children's Chorus, UNICEF)

1. We are the children of the world. No matter who our parents are, where we live, or what we believe, treat us as equals. We deserve the best the world has to give.

2. Protect us, so that we may grow in freedom and with dignity.

3. Let us each be given a name and have a land to call our own.

4. Keep us warm and sheltered. Give us food to eat and a place to play. If we are sick, nurse and comfort us.

5. If we are handicapped in body or mind, treasure us even more and meet our special needs.

6. Let us grow up in a family. If we cannot be cared for by our family, take us in and love us just the same.

7. Teach us well, so that we may lead happy and productive lives. But let us play, so that we may teach ourselves.

8. In times of trouble, help us among the first. The future of the world depends on us.

9. Protect us from cruelty and from those who would use us badly.

10. Raise us with tolerance, freedom, and love. As we grow up, we too will promote peace and understanding throughout the world.

Bibliography for Sources on Hunger

Children's Books

BAYLOR, BYRD. 1994. *The Table Where Rich People Sit*. New York: Charles Scribner's Sons. One of Baylor's seemingly simple picture books with a message about what being truly rich means.

GIKOW, LOUISE, and ELLEN WEISS. 1993. *For Every Child, a Better World*. New York: Muppet Press/Golden. This book illustrates many of the principles in the Declaration of the Rights of the Child and is dedicated to the memory of Audrey Hepburn.

KINDERSLEY, BARNABAS, and ANABEL KINDERSLEY. 1995. *Children Just Like Me*. London: Dorling Kindersley. Outstanding photographs. Within a standard format, children from around the world share their lives, dreams, and favorite things. Geography is personalized and information is shared in an engaging way. This book sets up a pattern that children in the classrooms can replicate to share information about themselves.

LEWIS, BARBARA. 1991. *The Kid's Guide to Social Action*. Minneapolis: Free Spirit Press. Steps that kids can take to solve social problems of their choice and turn creative thinking into positive action.

———. 1995. *The Kid's Guide to Service Projects*. Minneapolis: Free Spirit Press. Over five hundred service ideas for kids who want to make a difference.

MENZEL, PETER. 1994. *Material World: A Global Family Portrait*. San Francisco: Sierra Club Books. A beautifully photographed documentation of both the common humanity of the people of this planet and the great differences in material goods and circumstances that separate the rich and poor. Statistics support the revealing pictures. A CD-ROM is available for $59.95 at 1-800-782-7944. This book is a must for today's classroom.

ROSEN, MICHAEL J. 1994. *The Greatest Table: A Banquet to Fight Against Hunger.* New York: Harcourt Brace. A twelve-feet-long book illustrated by popular children's book artists and hosted by poet Michael Rosen specifically to aid Share Our Strength, an antihunger organization. The accordion format of this book provides a model for class or individual books.

Teacher Resources

Children Hungering for Justice and *World Food Day.* Curriculums for grades K–4 and 5–8 on hunger and children's rights. Church World Service, P.O. Box 968, Elkhart, IN 46515-0968, 219-264-3102. Three dollars each (free use of videos and audiovisuals upon request).

Coordinator, U.S. Committee for World Food Day, 1001 22nd Street NW, Washington, DC 20437, 202-653-2404. The source for a variety of educational and informational material related to World Food Day.

Famine and Chronic Persistent Hunger: A Life and Death Distinction. Videotape. The Hunger Project, 1388 Sutter Street, San Francisco, CA 94109, 415-928-8700. Free, and an outstanding presentation. Also available is an eight-lesson teacher's guide on ending hunger created by the Hunger Project and the National Council for the Social Studies.

Human Rights for Children Committee. 1992. *Human Rights for Children.* Alameda, CA: Hunter House. A curriculum for teaching human rights to children ages three through twelve. Partially funded by Amnesty International USA, this book has excellent teaching suggestions and solid bibliographies.

National Committee for World Food Day, 1776 F Street NW, Washington, DC 20437. Free curriculum (grades 4–7 and 8–12).

National Council of Returned Peace Corps Volunteers, 1319 F Street NW, #900, Washington, DC 20004, 202-393-5501. Returned volunteers are often uniquely qualified to bring information into our classrooms about hunger and other persistent global issues.

National Student Campaign Against Hunger and Homelessness, 29 Temple Place, Boston, MA 02111, 617-292-4823. A student-run action group that sponsors nationwide projects and campaigns, institutes innovative programs, and raises funds to educate the public and serve those in need.

Save the Children, 54 Wilton Road, Westport, CT 06880, 203-226-7271. Offers educational resources, including films.

U.S. Committee for UNICEF, 331 East 38th Street, New York, NY 10016. Nutrition/World Hunger kit, and Water, a Basic Need kit. About $8 each. These informational kits (there are kits available on other topics as well) provide excellent background information/pictures.

WILLIAMS, SONJA. 1987. *Exploding the Hunger Myths.* San Francisco: Food First/Institute for Food and Development Policy. A curriculum written for high school, but some parts are very useful for intermediate and middle school students. Contains excellent graphics for overheads and student discussions.

World Populations. Video. ZPG Publications, 1400 16th Street NW, Suite 320, Washington, DC 20036, 202-332-2200. Graphic simulation of the history of human population growth. About $30. Six minutes. Great for math, social studies, and science as well as hunger studies. Fantastic resource for all classrooms.

THREE

Across the United States: Creating a Collegial Classroom Community

Social studies programs should include experiences that provide for the study of people, places, and environments.

—NCSS Standard

It's important to build a collegial classroom community, not just among teachers within an individual classroom but among the kids in different classes within a grade level. There's been quite a bit of attention given to cross-age peer interaction but little to those groups of kids in the same grade who attend different classes. In intermediate and middle schools today, it's not unusual for a group of students to stay together most of the day. These students need to develop the ability to work with and appreciate people they don't know well.

We expect the kids in our classrooms to work with one another, and this goal is usually accomplished as the kids become familiar with one another's gifts and limitations. Once our students are relating this way, however, most of us relax and get on with it, thus missing an opportunity to provide authentic experiences and enrichment for our kids.

For instance, in our school, there are four fifth grades. A few years ago the four teachers met and talked about what we liked about our program and what we wanted to change. We liked the flexibility that allows two of us to maintain self-contained classrooms and two of us to departmentalize. We liked the open communication we have with one another. We liked the way we share resources and how we don't try to "one up" one another. But we were concerned about a relationship problem we saw developing among our classes. Each of us had experienced, at one time or another, a vague, almost invisible resistance from students in someone else's class.

This recalcitrant attitude often surfaced when one of us was attending to inappropriate behavior of fifth graders not in her classroom—those moments when one is on the fly, heading down to the copy machine or the storeroom and a kid is messing around in the hall. *Joann—or Julian—where are you supposed to be?* And Joann or Julian gives you "the look" that says, *You are not my teacher. Get off my case. Who are you to tell me what to do?*

We also felt, more than observed, an undercurrent of competition among the kids in the different classes. We wanted to replace these barely discernible group feelings with ones more positive and cooperative, and we identified the cause as not enough contact between one another's classes—the kids didn't feel a part of the cohesive whole we teachers felt we had achieved.

Creating a Cooperative Problem-Solving Unit

Our solution was to create a unit of study early in the year that brings the kids together in a culminating project in which they work with other teachers and with kids not in their own room, solving a problem cooperatively with a given set of materials in a limited amount of time. We shape this culminating project as an authentic learning experience, along the lines of what happens when we attend a community meeting and volunteer to serve on a committee, some or all of whose other members are strangers.

To build up to the culminating project, we undertake several activities—some group, some individual—in our regular classrooms. These activities integrate language arts, art, and geography.

We make geography of the United States the thematic base for the unit, but it could be geography of the world, ancient Africa, modern Canada, or any other place and still use similar activities and a similar culminating project. Throughout the unit, we present models and set standards that help the students learn how to create quality work, how to plan and complete a sequence of assignments, and, more generally, how to succeed in fifth grade by trying.

We deliberately build in what I call the "knows, dos, and feels" of learning. The *knows* are the heads-on academic skills students need. The *dos* are the hands-on products that demonstrate kids' ability to apply, synthesize, or evaluate the *knows*. The *feels* are the hearts-on attitudes and values we deliberately foster in the classroom to promote thoughtful citizenship for tomorrow. Translated into specifics, in this unit students:

- Think critically and creatively.
- Collaborate with others effectively.
- Communicate using multiple intelligences.
- Develop more competent research skills.
- Produce quality products as a result of their research.
- Demonstrate concern for others.

Beginning the Unit

We start this unit in our individual classrooms the second week of the new school year, when we are still setting up classroom routines and getting to know our students. We begin by accessing prior knowledge. In our school district, third graders study the geography of Washington State. They become familiar with common geographic references and with the symbols used in map legends and learn that maps are drawn to scale and that the scale can vary. Our fourth graders are introduced to the regions of the world by looking at specific communities within representative regions. They learn fundamental geographic concepts and skills, such as orienting a map, using scale to compute distance, interpreting map symbols, using a grid to locate places on a map or globe, and identifying landforms.

In fifth grade, we review these skills and see whether the kids can apply them to a new setting. I begin by passing out blank maps of the United States and asking the kids to fill in anything they know about the geography of our country without looking at a reference book or map. I'm not especially interested in states and cities but rather in geographic features, so I prompt with such statements as: *Don't forget major mountain ranges. Include the important rivers. Indicate bodies of water.*

When my kids are finished, they share their maps and then we compare them with a large topographical map of the United States. We celebrate the successful identifications and laugh over the distortions. Using the large map, I ask the students to decide how many regions there are in the United States and elicit some guesses about what might separate one region from another. Then I ask the students to indicate on their maps where they think different regions might be.

In small groups, the students take turns sharing their regional maps and we then examine why few had exactly the same regions. The reasons range from "different criteria" to "people had different ideas" to "depends on where you've been." I explain that this is true with adults and with textbooks as well. Different people or companies will identify different regions. As the students identify the regions from our text, which we have agreed to use as our authority, I ask volunteers to outline them on the wall map using an erasable marker or a piece of chalk.

Becoming Generalists

The students skim through the regions section of the social studies text and pick three regions in which they would be interested in specializing. Most of the regions comprise between five and seven states, and I tell them it will benefit some of our later work if no more students specialize in a region than there are states in the region; that way, there will be no more than one student per state. I then write the names of all the regions on the board or on an overhead, and the children narrow their choices to a single region to study further, switching to their second or third choice to even out the size of the groups.

Working in regional groups, the students begin collecting facts and information. Each group draws an outline of its region on a large piece of butcher paper and lists its "finds" there. This allows me to monitor group progress easily, and I spend time with groups that are having trouble. During this important research time we consult the text and books from the library and interview parents and friends. We separate facts from opinion, putting opinions in quotation marks. ("New York is the state where dreams come true" graces the map of Kendra, an aspiring actress.)

When the research phase is complete, each group presents their collection of information to the class. Our focus discussion question is, *How would we know we are in one region and not another region?* We leave the butcher paper lists on the wall as we move to more independent work.

Reading Across the United States

My students also read across the United States. I put up a large wall map and provide small sticky dots. During readers' workshop, when-

What Do You Know About the Mountain West Region?

ever a student reads a book from a recognizable location or region, he or she initials a dot and affixes it to the map in the proper place. I make sure our classroom library has picture books (Diane Siebert's *Mojave*, for example) and chapter books that discuss or are set in a definite geographic place. At first our goal was to read across the United States as a class, but several of the kids decided to try doing it by themselves or with a buddy. The picture books made this goal attractive and attainable.

My kids also keep personal maps in their journals on which they mark the sites, landmarks, and geographic features of the books they choose to read. (Some students come to my classroom hating to read because of the book report they must write when they finish. For these kids, being allowed to map their reading record is a welcome change.) The map they use identifies states, major mountain ranges, and major rivers and other bodies of water, so the kids are working with significant geographic features every day for more than a month. The kids also explain how the setting relates to or influences the story.

Layering the Multiple Intelligences

Good units deliberately blend in the multiple intelligences. Learning experiences are like the layers in an onion. Whether taking my lead from the kids or fashioning strategies to take them where they don't even know they want to go, I shape activities so that one experience is layered on another. These experiences gradually build into an integrated whole, or gestalt, from which the kids can draw analogies, apply skills, synthesize information, and evaluate problems.

Tourist Bureau Poster

Visual-spatial is usually the first intelligence I tap. Children who are not confident or skilled in linguistic mediums can often express themselves effectively through art. This is a perfect unit in which to integrate art skills. My instructions to the kids are to create a poster that the state's tourist bureau can use to promote tourism.

If I can, I invite a graphic artist into the classroom to show us the

I Like Max's Tourist Poster

techniques of effective poster design, thus deflecting the anxiety of those students who do not feel they are visually-spatially oriented and igniting the creativity of those who are. We learn about lettering. My kids are amazed to discover that outlining lettering in black enhances the potency of the message. They begin to see that keeping the design simple and uncluttered makes the message more memorable.

When our posters are complete, we talk about them, evaluating them according to the rubric in Appendix 3-1. Then we hang them around the room until they are used in the culminating project.

A Little Book of Alliteration
Another strategy the kids enjoy and learn a lot from is the little book of alliteration. Designed to appeal to the kinesthetic learner, this

strategy taps the visual-spatial, linguistic, and logical-mathematical intelligences as well.

I begin by reading a picture book to the class that includes clear examples of alliteration. My favorite one lately is *Away from Home* by Anita Lobel, with its multiple word and visual patterns.

After the students identify as many patterns in the book as they can, I ask them to work with a partner and make up an alliteration about Washington State using the same grammatical pattern as in the book. After an example or two, the kids usually take off, creating alliterative sentences galore. Keeping them appropriate can be a challenge. Frequent whole group sharing provides a way to monitor appropriateness and inspires as well.

Next I invite the students to create their own little book of alliteration about the state they are researching. I stress that I want their book to be about real places in their state, and we discuss where they can get information: a state map is best, an index is helpful, the Internet is time-consuming, interviews are a possibility.

First we fold a sheet of paper into a little book (see Appendix 2-3). Then I explain the format: cover page with title, author, and date; six pages of alliteration following the grammatical pattern established in the model (a proper noun, a verb and a two-word prepositional phrase ending in a proper noun—"Sally sang in Seattle") and using place names from their state; and a repeated visual pattern (color, shape) to frame the page. An added application is stated in the form of a challenge: *I challenge you to incorporate into your drawings physical features, plant or animal life, or historic landmarks that would be found in the vicinity of each place you mention in your alliterative sentences. For example, if the sentence is "Sally sang in Seattle," the accompanying illustration might have Puget Sound, Mount Rainier, or the Space Needle in the background.*

As we do with nearly everything, we share the books when we have finished. Usually we do this "round robin"—each child reads his or her neighbor's book, writes a comment on an accompanying piece of paper, and raises a hand to indicate readiness to trade. Kids continue to quietly read, write, and raise hands, trading their peers' books across the classroom. Since this is our first little book of the year, I want the kids to see the range, variety, and techniques their peers use so that they build a repertoire of ideas to incorporate into their own books next time. Each author and I then evaluate the book using the rubric in Appendix 3-2, and it is placed in the student's file and perhaps later in his or her portfolio.

Becoming Experts

Now it's time for the kids to investigate the geography and culture of the United States more specifically. It's also time to move to independent work. Each student has been asked to become an expert on a particular state. I choose this traditional focus for a couple of reasons. For one thing, most of the resources in our school revolve around information about individual states. For another, many of the kids want to know more about the state they, their parents, or their grandparents came from or they have a fantasy about visiting a particular state "just because it sounds neat." Of course, lots of kids want to pick Washington, because we live there and because they have studied it extensively in third grade. No way! They must choose another. Washington is mine!

We begin by discussing research writing. The students describe the purpose of research writing and how one goes about it. I get them to agree that the purpose is to inform based on fact, not opinion. I also make sure someone has mentioned that the writer often has an outline of what might be included and looks for information to flesh out the outline.

I ask the kids what they think is important to know about a state, listing their ideas on the board. The students' ideas usually fall under three major headings: general information (population, natural resources, climate, elevation), cultural information (history, famous people, places to visit), and economic information (chief products, manufacturing, agriculture). These three categories become our outline.

To set all the students up for success, I construct data sheets to help them collect and organize their research (see Appendix 3-3). I use Washington State as a model, walking the students through the data collection process. (A description of this process, along with examples, is in my book *Seeing the Whole Through Social Studies,* 182–84.)

This year we added the Internet as a resource. Yahoo is one source we dipped into (http://www.yahoo.com). It is more helpful for some states than for others. Global Network Navigator's Travel Center (http://www.gnn.com/gnn/meta/travel/res/countries.html) is another. Students can select region, country, state, or city, as they can on the http://www.city.net/ site.

There are many print resources available as well. In addition to encyclopedias, several publishers have state and country series. A series I particularly like is Hello U.S.A., published by Lerner Publications. The books are easy to read and very manageable for the less capable reader. This series is very student-friendly and sets up connections for time lines, science integration, and biographies later on.

Writing Using Research Data

Many students have a lot of experience writing creatively, but most of them have little experience with writing to share research. Most kids have a difficult time writing their own sentences when they are staring at a perfectly good sentence in an encyclopedia! Some uncontrollable urge says, *Copy it—even though Mrs. Lindquist says I shouldn't.* Solution? Remove the source. As my students wrap up their data collection, I clear the room of reference materials. I want them to work only from their notes.

I require a certain formality in the kids' research writing. The folksy approach many of them adopt in their creative writing isn't what we are after this time. Instead, they come bearing information that must be explained clearly. In writing about the state they have researched, they need to maintain the present tense most of the time, glancing backward occasionally to share a bit of history or moving forward to include some hints about the future.

Informational writers keep their material interesting. They don't load their sentences with long lists. They use transitions expertly, drawing the reader deeper into the piece. My students and I create a transitions chart, which we hang in the classroom for year-long reference. Words and phrases such as *therefore, however, on the other hand,* for example, at the same time, meanwhile, afterward, then, in the first place, finally, another, in addition, in fact, and nevertheless are featured on this chart. Informational writers always leave readers knowing at least one thing new and don't hit them over the head with things they probably already know. This means they may or may not use all their notes. Research-based writing is as much about what you decide not to use as it is about what you do use.

To model the process, I ask my students' help in creating a paragraph filled with general data regarding Washington State. We start by crafting an interesting topic sentence. Using the general data sheet, the class cooperatively dictates a meaty paragraph that usually turns out to be generic—and that's how I've designed it. The children can easily substitute data about their state. My goal is for all the students in my room to write a paragraph. This is their first informational writing in my classroom, and I don't want them to become discouraged. Most of the kids in my room use the paragraph simply as an example, but if a few use it as a crutch, that's okay with me this early in the year. Additionally, the information they are writing will help them with the cross-class collaboration near the end of the unit.

We walk through a couple of additional paragraphs in the same way. Each time fewer and fewer students replicate the model paragraph. The kids feel quite successful, and more important, they'll tackle their next writing assignment with a more positive outlook.

Editing by Peers

Any adult who does informational/research writing knows it's the rewriting that creates a piece worth reading. Most kids who have had experience with process writing would agree. However, when a child is rushed, editing doesn't happen. We have to decide how we are going to spend our class time and then commit to it. Kids don't edit everything they write in my classroom. Far from it. But there are some crucial experiences every year, and for my students writing from researched data and then editing what they have written is one of them. I use a format based on the Writing Northwest model, which was developed by Jim Sabol.

Before we start editing, my students word-process their paragraphs on the computer. They double-space, spell-check, and create as clean and accurate a draft as possible. A major benefit is that the kids do a lot of self-editing in the process. A second benefit is the ease with which the kids can make later editing changes.

Now the students pair up. One is designated *author*, the other, *editor*. The author reads her paper to the editor. The editor listens and enjoys. The author then pencils in any changes she wants and reads her paper again to the editor. This time the editor listens critically and suggests changes. The author makes the changes she agrees with. Now the two switch roles. The new author follows the same pattern of reading his paper aloud twice, correcting as wanted. Then the two switch papers, go to their desks, and correct any conventional errors they spot. When the papers are returned, it's quite easy for the author to go back to the computer and make corrections, additions, and deletions. (A peer editing guide is included in Appendix 3-4.)

Returning to the Beginning

Many teachers would be comfortable stopping here. Three or more solid paragraphs of research-based writing is not bad for a first try. However, at this point, I teach the kids about introductions and conclusions. Some argue that introductions should be taught earlier, before the students begin to write their research essay. But I do it here: now that we've written something, we have something to introduce.

Introductions to informational writing are tricky. They need to catch the reader's interest immediately. Freshness, humor, and surprise are beneficial: an unusual idea perhaps, or an interesting fact or question that captures the attention. Then the introduction must get to work, inform readers why the piece was written and why they ought to read it.

Once again, we write as a class. We come up with a riveting opening question or we reveal an interesting fact. We hook our reader. *Why is Washington called the Evergreen State? Maybe it's because of the rain that keeps everything green. Maybe it's because of the tall Douglas firs that cover the many mountains. Whatever the reason, Washington State is a beautiful place to visit.*

Finally, we move on to the conclusion. This type of paper normally calls for a summary, but summaries are difficult for young writers. So we write our conclusion based on a different criterion. I tell my students that they may use first- or second-person pronouns. I ask them to pretend they are the governor of their state and they are addressing the Tourist Directors of America's annual meeting. They must promote their state as an ideal tourist destination in order to bring in much-needed money for improvements that will benefit all the residents of the state. *Visitors always enjoy Washington State. They like the mountains for their beauty and quiet trails. They enjoy the desert landscape of the eastern part of the state. Easy access to lakes, rivers, Puget Sound, and the Pacific Ocean attracts water lovers. Washington is known as the Gateway to the Pacific, and visitors find they can travel to the Far East, Canada, or Hawaii easily. Come visit Washington State, where the people are friendly, the landscape is interesting, and the food is great! Don't forget to have a latte!*

We end up where we started, in the computer lab. Final drafts are word-processed. Covers are made, some electronically, others by hand. A bibliography is added. A final reflection and evaluation is thoughtfully submitted by every proud author. Each has developed a pool of knowledge about how to organize and write from research that we will dip into many more times during the year. Each has become an expert about a particular state in a specific region and has something to contribute to the success of the culminating project.

Meeting Basic Needs

Intermediate and middle-grade students are ready to test the concept that environment influences the way people satisfy their basic needs. While we should not teach students that geographic conditions determine how people live, they should learn that geography sets certain limits on the available choices (Jarolimek and Parker 1993, 137).

Most students have already studied native peoples, so I ask my students what they think is important to know about a culture. The discussion usually includes ways groups of people satisfy the basic needs of food, clothing, shelter, transportation, family life, and artifacts/weapons. Then I ask my students to research a Native American group within their state's region and find out how the group traditionally met its needs. They structure their research by folding a storyboard into eight panels. In the first panel they identify the title, author, and publication date of any source they consult. Panels two through seven are used to record whatever information they find. In the final panel they write a statement about what they learned. Once again, this activity provides another layer of knowledge for the culminating project.

We review how to use reference books, especially key words, alternative words, the index, and the table of contents. Web sites such as "Native American Experience, American Historical Images on File" are worth exploring (www.csulb.edulg/libarts/am-indian/nae/). We also look at picture books of lore, legends, and tales from Native American groups across the United States. I want to establish an appreciation for the richness and diversity of these cultures. I also want my students to begin to develop a critical eye regarding what is an accurate portrayal of native life and what is stereotyped.

When the storyboards are complete, the students share them within their regional groups. (The rubric we use to evaluate the storyboards in shown in Appendix 3-5.) Then I jigsaw the kids by region so everyone has an opportunity to look for similarities and differences among different geographic locations.

Just a Few Finishing Touches on the Data Storyboard

Making a Matrix

Some years I tap the logical-mathematical intelligence by asking the kids to create a matrix of the cultures they have researched. We list basic needs on one axis, the regions on the other, and the kids fill in the appropriate data. The information that gets plotted is impressive and revealing. Based on their accumulated knowledge, the kids then make generalizations about the geography of each region. They see clearly how environment and available resources shape culture.

I believe it is important to end our brief study of Native Americans by recognizing Native Americans in the present day. Thanks to authors such as Diane Hoyt-Goldsmith, we can bring contemporary Native Americans into our classrooms with some degree of integrity.

Drawing Pictorial Maps

Among the skills recommended for intermediate and middle-grade students in the National Council for the Social Studies standards document are the ability to orient a map, locate places, interpret map symbols, and express relative location. Drawing pictorial maps gives students the opportunity to practice all these skills. I ask my students to approximate the size, distance, and shape of their state or region, symbolize natural resources and chief products, and demonstrate an understanding of geographic features (see the project sheet in Appendix 3-6). Before they begin, I show them some examples. We discuss how pictorial maps are different from other maps they have seen, and we examine possible uses for these maps. The maps become part of the culminating project.

Concluding with Collaboration

The students are now ready to move on to the culminating project. Our goal is to create an authentic reason for kids to work collaboratively with children from other classrooms by solving a problem with limited resources and time. In the past three years, we've met this goal using two different but related strategies.

A colleague is a partner or association in the same office or place of work. To create the collegial part of our collaboration, we not only put our kids in cross-class groups but we have most kids work in different classrooms. We find that physically moving the kids into other classrooms promotes a sense of community and develops the working relationships between colleagues more quickly. As teachers we set the same expectations for work and behavior, taking full responsibility for kids temporarily assigned to our classrooms. *Starting today and for the next several days, you will be working in Mrs. Christoulis's, Mrs. Halverson's, or Mrs. Desimone's classrooms. Some of their students will be working with me. If you need materials or have any difficulties, see the teacher whose room you will be working in. Work hard and have fun!* (Kids, like most people, are resistant to the unknown, and that includes teachers and other kids. Nothing demystifies a teacher faster than working in his/her classroom! Nothing reveals a peer faster than working on the same project together. Doing this project at the beginning of the year develops a comfort zone for all our fifth graders so our kids easily come and go between our four classrooms.)

Look at This Pictorial Map

The Parade of States

In this project, the students work cooperatively and collaboratively to create a parade float featuring a specific state or region. The 120 students in our four classrooms are assigned to groups by the state they specialized in. (In most cases, three or four students have chosen the same state. Students who have chosen a state that no one else has selected form regional groups.) They come together with a common interest and similar information and are given a limited amount of time in which to complete the float, approximately five hours.

We provide the same materials to all the groups: two or three large pieces of tag board, crepe paper, butcher paper, construction paper, tissue paper, tempera paint, staplers, and masking tape. The groups can bring the following items from home, if they wish: cardboard, wire, foil, balloons, wrapping paper, wood, foam, paper napkins, paper plates, and spray paint. (They may use the spray paint only under close teacher supervision, however.)

Each group also needs to provide a wagon, wheelbarrow, trike, or bike—something to make the float mobile. Our final rule is that no group may spend more than two dollars purchasing materials.

We introduce this activity on a Friday and give the groups time to meet and do some preliminary planning. One of the major problems the kids must solve is, *How do we construct the float so it stays intact as we circle the school for the Parade of States?* We outline the work schedule so the kids see how much time they have and give them a rubric (see Appendix 3-7) so they are clear on the criteria. Ideas percolate all weekend, and by Monday afternoon most groups are ready to begin construction.

The groups work on their floats for four afternoons, and we have our Parade of States on Friday. Rather than disrupt the school hallways, we parade around the outside walkways of the school building. The kids also parade across the stage in our multipurpose room, for parents and each other. Each group introduces themselves and points out highlights of their float. They end their brief presentation with a statement about one thing they learned from this activity, one thing they liked, and one thing they'd change. Cameras are much in evidence, and the kids enjoy one another's finished products. The teachers fill out the evaluation rubric and comment orally on each group's work.

A "States" Fair

The project here is to create a booth at a fair informing people about a state (or region) in a memorable way. Once again, we establish groups of children by state or region, from all our different classes. Once again, the kids complete several activities as a way of showing themselves and us what they know: the requirements this time are one three-dimensional representation of a product from or natural resource of the state, a song or jingle about the geography of the state, and a visual-spatial-oral presentation discussing landmarks, historical events, and cultural features. Once again, we maintain control of the materials and time given for the cross-class groups to create the booths and prepare the information.

This project taps more skills than the Parade of States. First, a deeper and broader understanding of the state is required for the kids to be able to synthesize their knowledge into the required displays. Second, the kids use oral communication skills as they inform guests about their state. Finally, they need to be self-disciplined and more skilled at working cooperatively, because the "states" fair lasts about two and a half hours and over five hundred people attend, ranging in age from prekindergartners to grandmas and grandpas. Staying in the booth and staying on task are big challenges for some.

Speaking Persuasively

The final activity in our Across the United States unit is an independent one—a persuasive speech, so the kids have the opportunity to use the knowledge they have acquired throughout our study in their own unique ways. *You have recently been elected governor of your state. At the annual Conference of Governors you will have an opportunity to address the Tourist Directors of America about why your state is so special and why others should visit it. This is a very important speech, because many people in your state are out of work. Tourists could mean new jobs and new opportunities for these folks. As the new governor, you recognize that this is a very important opportunity.*

The students recognize the similarity of this activity to the research they did earlier. The similarity is deliberate. I want my students to review their research papers as they create their speeches. I want to reinforce that research is useful.

I ask the students to help develop criteria for an oral presentation. Their ideas about what skills should be incorporated into a good speech usually fall into two main categories: mechanics and content. Each year we come up with a rubric similar to the one shown in Appendix 3-8.

Ready for the State's Fair to Start

Before the students begin working, we brainstorm how one might put together such a speech. The kids' suggestions often include: *Use all the past projects for information. Write it out. Just make notes. Say it over and over to yourself. Don't wait till the last minute. Decide if you want a visual aid or a prop. Ask a friend to listen and make comments.*

Focusing on the speeches for short periods of class time is more productive than doing so for longer periods. About ten minutes at a time works best. Giving students a weekend to practice increases success. Giving them a choice about when they will present their speech increases their comfort level, so my students indicate which of the three consecutive days they prefer, and we resolve any conflicts by drawing names out of a hat. Some kids dress up. Some bring in visual aids. Some invite their "team" mates in from the other classrooms to help. Each presentation reflects the depth and breadth of their learning.

Adding Poetry

Most of my students find that making the speech last long enough is very difficult. I tell them that one way to stretch a speech without having it lose momentum or interest is to add some appropriate poetry. Since we are studying the geography of the United States and tuning in to related historical events, we search for poetry in those categories.

Recently, some excellent books have been published that help my students find appropriate poetry for speeches extolling the natural wonders and the history of specific states or regions. One is *Celebrate America in Poetry and Art*, edited by Nora Panzer and published by the National Museum of American Art. Another is *Celebrating America: A Collection of Poems and Images of the American Spirit*, compiled by Laura Whipple. Both of these books provide students with poetry that presents a geographic perspective (Carl Sandburg's "Niagara," Emily Dickinson's "To Make a Prairie" [Poem 1755], and Hamlin Garland's "A Dakota Wheatfield," for example) or a historical perspective (Rosemary and Stephen Vincent Benét's "Western Wagons" and Ralph Waldo Emerson's "Concord Hymn," for example).

This strategy introduces the students to poetry in an authentic context and is a technique good speakers often use. I demonstrate weaving poetry into a presentation, beginning with an excerpt from a poem that sets the tone or catches the attention, inserting a line or two of poetry into the middle of my speech, and using lines from a poem to end my presentation effectively. These models are very important. Just talking about something seldom works with my kids. And not only do I demonstrate, but we discuss each demonstration, identifying what was happening as well as how I did it.

Endnote

Since we started the deliberate fostering of collegial classrooms, the climate of our grade level has improved. The "look" has been replaced by a good-natured smile when students' behavior requires a prompt from one of the teachers from outside the classroom. Kids comfortably pass back and forth between classrooms, running errands, borrowing materials, or just stopping by to see what's happening. We've really noticed a change on the field trips when more than one class is together. We are more of a unit. Fewer disturbances occur. Kids look forward to working with one another again. Recently, we put on a grade level operetta. Ninety percent of the fifth-grade kids gave up their recesses to rehearse and perform. While the production was excellent, what everyone was really impressed with was the cohesive spirit and supportive climate the kids generated onstage. A community has been established where we are all connected and where we all care about one another.

Appendix 3-1: Rubric for Evaluating a Poster

1. Criterion: attractive

1	3	5
not yet	caught my attention	can't forget it

Indicators: colorful, easy to read, simple, neatly done, effective layout

2. Criterion: informative

1	3	5
not very	somewhat	outstanding

Indicators: accurate, memorable, interesting

3. Criterion: creative

1	3	5
budding	blossoming	blooming

Indicators: original, dramatic, inventive

Appendix 3-2: Rubric for Little Book of Alliteration

1. Criterion: provides pattern of alliteration

1	3	5
not yet	inconsistent	consistent

2. Criterion: establishes a visual pattern

1	3	5
not yet	inconsistent	consistent

3. Criterion: establishes word pattern

1	3	5
not yet	inconsistent	consistent

4. Criterion: uses real place names

1	3	5
not yet	inconsistent	consistent

5. Criterion: uses time in class wisely

1	3	5
not yet	inconsistent	consistent

6. Criterion: Incorporates recognizable physical features, plant/animal life, or historic landmarks accurately

1	3	5
not yet	inconsistent	consistent

Comments:

Appendix 3-3: Across the U.S. Data Sheet Model

YOUR NAME Marion

GENERAL DATA

CAPITAL: HonoLuLu

AREA IN SQUARE MILES: 6,450 sq.

47th in size

ELEVATION:
HIGHEST: Mauna Keay
13,796 ft.
LOWEST: Sea Level

STATE GOVERNMENT:
NUMBER OF REPRESENTATIVES: 51

NUMBER OF STATE SENATORS: 25

2 us senators 2 us Representatives

CHIEF PRODUCTS: Cattle, dairy products, canned fruits and vegies, sugar, Tuna.

POPULATION: 1975 865,000

40th Among the States

STATE ABBREVIATIONS: H I

STATE TREE: Kukui

STATE FLOWER: Hibiscus

STATE MOTTO: Ua Mau he ea o Ka aina i ka Pono

STATE BIRD: Nene (Hawaii goose)

STATE SONG: Hawaii Ponoi

LAND REGIONS:

Hawaii
Maui
KahooLawe
Lanai
Oahu
Kauai
Niihau

CLIMATE:

HIGHEST TEMPERATURE: 100°F

LOWEST TEMPERATURE: 14°F

RAINFALL (PRECIPITATION):

10 inches
Average annual
temperature 75°F

Appendix 3-4: Peer Editing Guide

Editor:

Author:

First Reading (by the author): Listen and enjoy

Second Reading (by the author): Did you hear:

1. The purpose of each paragraph (topic sentence)?
2. Voice?
3. Transitions?
4. Consistent tense?

Third Reading (silently by editor):

1. Conventions:

    A. Paragraphs indented? (use an arrow)
    B. Complete sentences? (indicate problem by using "Inc.")
    C. Proper punctuation? (indicate problem by adding or deleting)
    D. Spelling correct? (circle all questionable spellings)

2. Content:

    A. Makes sense? (Ideas clear? Organization easy to follow?)
    B. Interesting? (Sentences fluent? Words work well?)
    C. Feels finished? (Reader satisfied?)

Compliment Sandwich: One thing I liked . . .
                       One thing you might change . . .
                       Another thing I liked . . .

Appendix 3-5: Rubric for Storyboard About Native Americans

1. Criterion: visual presentation

1	3	5
room to grow	attractive	WOW!

2. Criterion: effective research skills

1	3	5
missing info	some inaccuracies	accomplished

3. Criterion: demonstrates insight into culture

1	3	5
not yet	some evidence	much evidence

Appendix 3-6: Pictorial Map Project Sheet

You have just been hired by the tourist bureau to create an attractive map to entice visitors to your state. You have been instructed that this map should:

1. Identify and outline the state, indicating bordering states or bodies of water.
2. Indicate population density.
3. Indicate chief products and natural resources with symbols.
4. Identify major geographic features (mountains, rivers, lakes, etc.).
5. Include a legend.
6. Draw in a compass rose showing the orientation of it on your map.

Your employers have made it very clear that this map should be colorful, attractive, easy to read, and relatively accurate. Good luck. Your deadline is seven days from today. You will have ample class time in which to prepare it.

Appendix 3-7: Rubric for the Parade-of-States Float

1. State/region identified or symbolized

   smattering of applause   round of applause   standing ovation

2. Creative

   smattering of applause   round of applause   standing ovation

3. Colorful

   smattering of applause   round of applause   standing ovation

4. Aesthetically pleasing/interesting

   smattering of applause   round of applause   standing ovation

5. Mobile and stays intact during the parade

   smattering of applause   round of applause   standing ovation

6. Completed within time given

   smattering of applause   round of applause   standing ovation

7. Demonstrated wise use of materials

   smattering of applause   round of applause   standing ovation

8. Group cleaned up after each session and at end of the project

   smattering of applause   round of applause   standing ovation

9. Members demonstrated cooperation within the group

   smattering of applause   round of applause   standing ovation

Appendix 3-8: Rubric for Governor's Speech

	Not Yet		Sometimes	Outstanding	
Mechanics:					
Makes eye contact	1	2	3	4	5
Speaks loudly and clearly	1	2	3	4	5
Is at least 1.5 minutes long	1	2	3	4	5
Body/voice are expressive	1	2	3	4	5
Content:					
Gets attention	1	2	3	4	5
Conveys information	1	2	3	4	5
Uses a variety of words	1	2	3	4	5
Ends with a clincher	1	2	3	4	5

Bibliography for Literature on Geography

CASSIDY, JOHN. 1994. *Earthsearch: A Kids' Geography Museum in a Book.* Palo Alto, CA: Klutz Press. More exhibit than book, the three-dimensional pages invite the reader to a hands-on exploration of geography terms, concepts, and topics. In addition to being a resource for creating a geography museum in the classroom, the book invites students to assemble their own pages of hands-on geography. Kids love the aluminum cover of the book made from a Russian Coca-Cola can.

CHERRY, LYNNE. 1992. *A River Ran Wild: An Environmental History*. Orlando, FL: Harcourt Brace. Each illustration in this pictorial history of a river from an environmental point of view provides information about the geography of the Nasua River region and insights into how human technology can make or break natural conditions. I use this as a model and my kids create their own pages using the pattern established in the book.

———. 1994. *The Armadillo from Amarillo*. Orlando, FL: Harcourt Brace. In addition to presenting geographic features from a variety of visual perspectives, this picture book is also a model for how to use postcards to highlight the physical features of a region and add a personal point of view.

CIMENT, JAMES, with RONALD LAFRANCE. 1996. *Encyclopedia of the North American Indian*. New York: Scholastic. This book includes information about 143 groups of American Indians, in alphabetical order. Eleven regions are also listed alphabetically. Indian groups are portrayed in three time frames: past, present, and future. This is an important new resource, easy to read and easy to use.

Hello U.S.A. (series). 1993. Minneapolis: Lerner. Each book in this series is devoted to a single state and includes the following chapters: Did You Know?, A Trip Around [State], [State]'s Story, Living and Working in [State], and Protecting the Environment. The books are easy to read and very manageable for the less capable reader. Also included are a historical time line, introductions to famous people from the state, facts-at-a-glance, and a pronunciation guide and glossary. The series is very student-friendly and sets up connections for time lines, environmental integration, and biographies later on.

HOYT-GOLDSMITH, DIANE. 1991. *Pueblo Storyteller*. New York: Holiday House. Engaging photographs and text revealing the life and customs of a ten-year-old Pueblo storyteller. This book helps my kids separate the traditional and contemporary life of one Southwest Native American. It also helps them understand the geography of the region. Hoyt-Goldsmith presents a similar treatment of present-day Northwest Coastal Indians in her book *Totem Pole*.

LATROBE, KATHY HOWARD, series ed. 1994. Exploring the United States Through Literature. Phoenix, AZ: Oryx.

FREY, P. DIANE, ed. *Exploring the Northeast States Through Literature.*

VELTZE, LINDA, ed. *Exploring the Southeast States Through Literature.*

LATROBE, KATHY HOWARD, ed. *Exploring the Great Lakes States Through Literature.*

BRODIE, CAROLYN S., ed. *Exploring the Plains States Through Literature.*

SHARP, PAT TIPTON, ed. *Exploring the Southwest States Through Literature.*

SMITH, SHARYL, ed. *Exploring the Mountain States Through Literature.*

COLL, CAROL A., ed. *Exploring the Pacific States Through Literature.*

Each of these books is first organized by the states within the region. Each state section is then subdivided into nonfiction, biography (collective and then individual), fiction, periodicals, and finally, professional materials. Each bibliography entry includes Dewey classification number, ISBN or ISNN, date of publication or release, number of pages, black-and-white or color illustrations, cost of nonprint materials, any special purchasing information, and running time and format specifications for nonprint items. Each entry also includes an interest-level designation and relevant subject headings. Each volume contains an extensive directory of publishers and vendors who could be contacted via mail or Internet.

LOBEL, ANITA. 1994. *Away from Home.* New York: Greenwillow. Charming ABC picture book that uses alliteration to describe its globe-trotting characters. This book is a strong model for teaching alliteration, parts of speech, and visual patterns.

PANZER, NORA, ed. 1994. *Celebrate America in Poetry and Art.* New York: Hyperion. This book is heavily tied to the geography of the United States and is published in association with the National Museum of Art, Smithsonian Institution. I particularly like the poetry selections, which are very appealing to kids. The artwork adds another dimension of comprehension.

ROBBINS, KEN. 1994. *Water.* New York: Henry Holt. In this stunning photographic essay on the varied geology of the United States, Robbins combines art with information. The simple text reveals complex concepts. This is one of four books, the others being *Earth, Wind,* and *Fire.* Handsome color and black-and-white photographs feature the terrain and the landmarks of this country.

SIEBERT, DIANE. 1989. *Heartland.* New York: HarperTrophy. Sparse text and dramatic illustrations by Wendell Minor invite every reader into the very essence of the Midwest. One reading of the book fills your mind's eye with delight. A second reading makes you feel as though you've been there. Siebert has also collaborated with the same artist on *Mojave* and *Sierra.*

SIS, PETER. 1993. *A Small Tall Tale from the Far Far North.* New York: Knopf. My favorite Sis book. Not only does the reader learn about Inuit people and how they live on their land, but Sis uses several patterns that can be replicated by kids in constructing their own books.

WHIPPLE, LAURA, compiler. 1994. *Celebrating America: A Collection of Poems and Images of the American Spirit.* New York: Philomel. American history and geography are beautifully blended in this collection of poems and artwork provided by the Art Institute of Chicago. This book helps me integrate poetry in my curriculum in very natural ways.

FOUR

Trade Fair: Orchestrating a One-Period Peak Experience

Social studies programs should include experiences that provide for the study of how people organize for the production, distribution, and consumption of goods and services.

—NCSS Standard

Getting Ready

Dear Parent(s),

Your child is going to be studying exploration and colonization this trimester. One of the activities that brought early Europeans and Native peoples together was trade. Money wasn't used: wares or goods were. To give the children in my classroom a clearer understanding of trading and bartering, we are going to have a trade fair. Two weeks from today the children should bring some hand-crafted or homemade wares to school. These wares should be inexpensive, made primarily from things found around your home or neighborhood. Examples of wares students have made in the past for this activity include friendship bracelets, stationery, cookies, bookmarks, pressed flowers, and clay beads. The children can bring as many or as few items as they like, but they must bring something. Your child should do the work involved in making the items and should clean up any resulting mess.

Thanks for your support.

Sincerely,
Mrs. L

Advance notice is necessary to make this activity work. I need to help parents learn to schedule time for school as much as I need to help my students manage homework assignments. Many of my students' parents are so busy that they have little time for motivating and supervising the completion of work done at home. The home-school link is stretched so taut these days, I tend my relationships carefully, providing plenty of advance notice for projects that require extra support. Nothing incites a parent's resentment faster than having a child pipe up at 9:00 P.M., "Oh Mom, guess what? I have to make a [blank], take in a [blank], create a [blank] for school tomorrow."

The parents of students in my class receive three notices about this project. I give the first one orally in September, when we meet during curriculum night. During my overview of the year, I emphasize this "coming attraction." In my October parent letter, I mention the trade fair briefly, encouraging parents to begin exploring with their children possible things they can make. The letter above goes out the first of November. We have completed our study of the early colonies by this point and are about to move on to the events leading up to the Revolutionary War. Making wares will be the only homework assignment for the second week in November.

We also talk about the upcoming trade fair in class. We comb the libraries to find pictures of people trading and information about marketplaces from many cultures and time periods. We share our personal experiences with trading and bartering. We brainstorm possible products to create. And we plan, discussing how each of us has nights that are less busy than other nights and how to make time for this kind of assignment. We estimate how much time it takes to make something—a friendship bracelet, for example—and then how much time one would have to carve out during a series of evenings or a weekend in order to make five of the items. Since every child is required to participate, it's important to build a number of scenarios that illustrate diverse ways of making things at home and having them ready on the designated day.

Trading Day

On the day of the trade fair, the kids bring in their wares. I encourage them to keep the items under wraps initially, so we can begin the day as usual and surprise one another later. I find the best time to hold the fair is after the morning recess. That way, if children have forgotten their wares or simply didn't make any, I can help them make something quickly during recess. (Bookmarks are the quickest: using a paper cutter and some stickers from a recent book club order, voilà!)

Ready for the Trade Fair

After recess, my kids reposition their desks to form a square around the edges of the room, simulating a marketplace. Then each child stands up and displays the wares he or she has brought. Some kids bring a lot: dozens of cookies, bags of popcorn, plastic sacks of peanut brittle. Others bring only a few of an item: hair decorations, paper dolls, little origami boxes, balls made of rubber bands.

Next, I have the kids practice saying "no thank you." The hardest part of trading and bartering is refusing an offer, so we practice how to refuse nicely. The role-playing is quick, effective, and instructive:

"Hi, want to trade?"

"No, thanks, I already have enough of that."

"Hey, how about giving me that for this?"

"Um, I don't think so. I don't really need it. Thanks anyway."

"I'll give you three of these for one of that."

"No, thanks. But I'll take four of those and one of that."

"Huh-uh, that's too much. But thanks for the offer. See ya."

Finally, the rules and regulations: *Take nothing off anyone's desk. You must be handed the wares by the owner. Some of you will be more comfortable staying at your desks and waiting for traders to come to you. Others will want to roam around the room, trading. Your desk is your private property. No one can take anything from your desk. Remember to be considerate and have fun!*

This for That

Trading usually begins with the "popular" group clustering around each other, sharing their wares and making quick trades. The fringe kids, the ones who are shy, who lack self-confidence, or who simply like to look things over first, watch. Within a few minutes, however, the circle of trading begins to enlarge, like the concentric circles on a pond when a rock is thrown in. It doesn't take long for every child to be actively engaged in trading and bartering. John brought cookies.

Will You Take This for That?

He trades a cookie for a bookmark. He trades another cookie for a painted rock. He soon discovers that he can trade his newly acquired bookmark and three cookies for a much coveted friendship bracelet.

This kind of activity needs to be cut off before the kids get tired of it. A half hour is about the longest they can sustain it. So after about twenty or twenty-five minutes, I blink the lights and announce that trading is over. The kids beg, "Just five more minutes" and begin a trading frenzy. Bargains abound. Deals are fast and furious. The marketplace is abuzz.

Trading does close at the end of five minutes. I have my kids sit down and spend a few moments just looking at the goods they've acquired and thinking about what just happened.

Wrapping Up

Debriefing links learning with experience. It is the most important part of the activity from my point of view as a teacher. I want to build

So, What Did You Observe During the Trade Fair?

a personal analogy for each child, a personal pool of knowledge he or she can draw from later on. This knowledge pertains to the basic law that operates in a free-market economy, the law of supply and demand. I begin by asking the kids, "What just happened?"

The discussion that follows reveals what the children have done, what they've learned, and how they feel about it. They recount their experience: "I had a lot of cookies and Susan only had three necklaces. Everyone wanted her necklaces. I had to work hard to trade my cookies." As the children talk, I restate their observations, using new vocabulary: "So you had a large supply and Susan didn't. You noticed there was more demand for Susan's product than yours. How come?"

It doesn't take long before we are all using words like *supply, demand,* and *scarcity.* We are able to discuss two basic economic ideas—people generally have unlimited wants, and the world offers limited resources—and apply these concepts to the trade fair. It dawns on the kids that the laws we are talking about are not rules that must be obeyed but are "laws" in the scientific sense, generalizations that accurately describe a large number of events. This brief but unforgettable, or peak, experience sets the stage for later, more detailed explorations into the world of economics.

Individual Reflections

After the informal, on-the-spot debriefing, it is important to have each child reflect about the experience on paper. I use a couple of different strategies to encourage this reflection in my classroom. One is the newspaper-in-a-day technique I describe in *Seeing the Whole Through Social Studies* on pages 62 and 63. Another is the quartile strategy.

Quartiles are folded books that can be made quickly out of notebook paper. A way to elicit thoughtful responses from students, a quartile is a perfect ending to an exciting activity. Not too lengthy or time-consuming but nevertheless revealing and retrospective, the quartile can be used many times in the classroom.

I ask my kids to take out a piece of notebook paper, fold it in half horizonally, and then fold it in half again vertically, creating a four-page book—hence the term *quartile* (thanks to Valerie Welk for this idea). On the first page the kids write the title of the activity, the date, and their name; on the next page, they write about what they did; on the third page, they write about what they learned; on the back page, they write about what they feel.

Because folding the paper is intriguing, kids share more readily and fully than if I had said to them, *Okay class, take out a piece of lined notebook paper and write three quarters of a page about what we just experienced.* An assignment like that would have ruined the experience for some kids. But fold a quartile, set a specific objective for each page (*do, know, feel*), and it's not unusual to have kids ask, May I write more?

From the Horses' Mouths

What Did You Do?

When I made the cookies it was easy. When I stuck the frosting on, I had help from my mom. But sticking the sprinkles on was simple. When I traded, I just went from desk to desk, asking for one of those for one of these. Next time I would make different things.

—Kelsey

I Love the Trade Fair!

Today I traded NBA predictions. Most of the trades I did involved food or bracelets. At one point I had eleven Rice Krispy treats!

—Brad

For the trade fair, I brought a bean-bag toss, three bean bags, a little fake baseball, and a modeling clay figure. I went around trying to get a stress squeezer. In the end I got one by making IOU bean bags.—Stephen

I started out with eighteen items and I got seven new ones. I made pins, bookmarks, bracelets, and rings. The new treasures I got were two pretty pins, a cotton-ball dog, clip-on earrings, NBA predictions (yuk!), and a colored rope. I was very happy with what I got.—Anonymous

I started making stuff this morning. I think I got a good deal because I started with five sand dollars and ended up with ten bags of peanut brittle and three brownies. I traded all my stuff, mostly for peanut brittle.—Craig

What Did You Learn?

I learned sometimes you have to give a person time to think about if they want to trade their things or not. Sometimes people don't really think. They just say yes and give you what you want and take what you trade them.—Kelsey

Today I learned to wait awhile before I trade. If I had to do it all over again, I'd not get as much food. And Mrs. L., don't be surprised if I'm not at school tomorrow. I think I ate too much. I'd also be a better waiter. I think I could've got better items.—Brad

If my class had another trade fair, there are a few things I would change. The main thing would be to work on the things all throughout the assignment. This time I waited until the last minute. I probably could have made better items.—Stephen

I learned the most rare things there were the most sought after. Once the creator of the treasures realized how low-priced their objects were, they made their prices higher. One person realized his treasures were so valuable that he decided not to trade at all!
—Anonymous

I learned that you want to trade for stuff that will go up in popularity because then you can trade those items for more. I learned to bargain. Next time I will bring items that were popular this time. I learned to try to get the best deal rather than just say yes to your best friend and get a bad deal.—Craig

How Do You Feel?

When I first said no thanks, I felt kinda sad. But then I realized that everyone was saying no thanks. So I didn't feel so bad when I said no. I didn't really care much when people said no. I just went to someone else. I sorta got mad sometimes because someone wouldn't leave me alone even though I said no.—Kelsey

Right now I feel sick, like I said, I ate too much.—Brad

I feel like my trading at the trade fair was a success. I got what I really wanted. I also got a neat femo bracelet. It doesn't fit me, but I think it looks nice. I was a little unhappy with my claymation pitcher, Mr. Abuse. It didn't trade for anything. I like it, though.

—Stephen

I feel that this trade fair was full of deals. Some people waited until a really good offer came. Others ran after one another to find a good deal. Me? I really ran after others to find a good deal.

—Anonymous

I felt happy after I was done trading, because I had got a good trade, in my opinion. I also feel sad because I felt I had ripped the other people I traded with off. I feel that next time I will do better. Before the trade fair I thought no one would want my items but I guessed wrong.—Craig

Endnote

Kids love the trade fair. They want to do it more than once because they learn so much the first time. They can see the relationship between supply and demand. They are canny in their ability to problem-solve. (One of my kids gave IOUs for goods he didn't have but promised to deliver. And he did!)

Teachers love the trade fair. Eighth-grade teachers tell me that their students have so much fun and write perceptive papers afterward about how trade influences relations between people. Fourth-grade teachers marvel at the skill with which their kids make their trades. Sixth- and seventh-grade teachers have written me about their success, often commenting on how this activity brings out the shy students and provides a venue for "new" kids to become participating classroom members.

Teachers also love the trade fair because it acts as a springboard for further study in economics. It's quite easy to move from the laws of supply and demand to the factors of production (natural resources, labor, capital goods, and entrepreneurship). Whether studying about manufacturing and industries or services such as transportation, sales, banking, education, and entertainment, the kids can relate back to the trade fair, making connections that have reality for them.

Bibliography for Trade Through the Ages

FRITZ, JEAN, MARGARET MAHY, PATRICIA MCKISSACK, FREDRICK MCKISSACK, KATHERINE PATERSON, and JAMAKE HIGHWATER. 1992. *The World in 1492*. New York: Henry Holt. A 1993 Children's Book of Distinction. Children's storytellers and history scholars have written chapters on Europe, Asia, Africa, Australia and Oceania, and the Americas. Each chapter is illustrated with maps, drawings, period artifacts, and works of art, making an important contribution to multicultural understanding, not only of trade between people, but of their lives and accomplishments as well.

HAWKE, SHARRYL DAVIS, and JAMES E. DAVIS. 1992. *Seeds of Change: The Story of Cultural Exchange After 1492*. Menlo Park, CA: Addison Wesley. An engagingly written paperback book rich in facts, illustrations, and artifacts. It is based on the exhibit "Seeds of Change" held at the National Museum of Natural History in Washington, D.C., to mark the five hundredth anniversary of Columbus' arrival in the Bahamas. It represents the life's work of scholars around the world as they have interpreted the true meaning of Columbus' voyage. Especially useful to those teachers who want to use the *concept* of exploration to guide their planning rather than the *theme* of exploration.

KALMAN, BOBBIE. 1992. *Early Stores and Markets*. New York: Crabtree. An inexpensive paperback about the development of commerce in colonial America. Easily read information for the beginning researcher.

LANGLEY, ANDREW, and PHILIP DESOUZA. 1996. *The Roman News*. Cambridge, MA: Candlewick. A wonderfully engaging "newspaper" reflecting Roman life from 800 B.C. to A.D. 400 and filling the reader in on the news and the lifestyles of the people. Several pages are devoted to trade and commerce, and they include excellent maps showing worldwide trade routes and valued products.

LORENZ, ALBERT, with JOY SCHLEH. 1996. *Metropolis: Ten Cities, Ten Centuries*. New York: Harry N. Abrams. A rich book in every sense of the word: rich in content, rich in illustrations, and rich in creativity. You could give this book to every teacher and student you know, because it will fascinate and inform any reader, regardless of age or interest.

MACDONALD, FIONA, and GERALD WOOD. 1996. *Exploring the World*. New York: Peter Bedrick. The Spice Islands are finally placed in context in this book, which features two epic journeys: those of Ferdinand Magellan and Sir Francis Drake. The impact these first two circumnavigations of the globe had on politics, geographical knowledge, and international trade is clearly and simply told.

MARTELL, HAZEL MARY. 1995. *The Kingfisher Book of the Ancient World: From the Ice Age to the Fall of Rome*. New York: Kingfisher. An easily read narrative of facts, figures, and fascinating information combined with illustrations and photographs. Perfect for the reluctant reader. Excellent glossary, chronology, and index. Impressive information on trade across cultures and time.

MASON, ANTONY. 1996. *If You Were There: Medieval Times*. New York: Simon & Schuster Books for Young Readers. Emphasizing the development of trade and government during the Middle Ages, this book provides insights into the living conditions and values of this period of history with charming illustrations and facts sure to appeal to the middle school researcher.

MILLARD, ANNE. 1993. *How People Lived*. London: Dorling Kindersley. Yet another of the excellent references published for young researchers and their teachers by this company. Especially useful for the trade fair unit is the section titled "Market Day in Athens."

PARTRIDGE, ELIZABETH. 1996. *Clara and the Hoo Doo Man*. New York: Dutton Children's Books. The only chapter book in this bibliography featuring trade and bartering, this is a charming new story about bartering goods for services in 1900. Clara always seems to find ways to worry her mother in their home near Red Owl Mountain, Tennessee, but when her younger sister is near death, Clara risks seeking the help of the herbal healer her mother calls the hoo doo man. This story is based on a real incident in the life of an African American woman.

POWELL, ANTON, and PHILIP STEELE. 1996. *The Greek News*. Cambridge, MA: Candlewick. Like *The Roman News* this book uses the newspaper approach to engage young readers in the great events in Greek history, along with adding fascinating facts about everyday life. "Trade News" is a feature article written in a way that will intrigue and interest youthful readers.

FIVE

Cooperative Biographies: Focusing on Reading, Research, Writing, and Responsibility

Social studies programs should include experiences that provide for the study of individual development and identity.

—NCSS Standard

Question: What Did You Learn from Writing a Cooperative Book?

I learned that not everyone in the group will do their share. I learned that I really sometimes like doing books. I learned that I see the other side of people I work with.—Kisa

I learned that it is easier to write a cooperative book than a book by yourself. It's fun to work in a group. You can make your book a lot longer.—James

I learned how to use a computer.—Scott

That you need to compromise a lot. You work hard and do many drafts of the story. It takes a lot of time.—Sarah

That you can't do whatever you want; otherwise it won't work. You have to listen to other people because they might have a better idea than you. And you can't get mad and then not talk because then you'll really have a bad product.—Julia

What it was like in those days. Abe had a very full life. It can be hard putting all the parts together.—Laura

I learned that if a group works together, it can turn out good. I learned that if you think, you can lengthen your chapter a lot. I learned that I'm a good note taker.—Ken

A Gift

Cooperative biographies came to me as a gift from two people, Walter C. Parker and Myra Zarnowski. Walter I know well; Myra I have never met. Yet these two people collaborated in the way educators all over the globe work together, often without knowing it, to enrich a number of other people—like me and my students.

I was attending an after-school inservice, not unusual. But I was crashing an inservice in an adjoining district, perhaps a little unusual. (I remember trying to make myself invisible.) I wanted very much to hear the invited speaker, Walter C. Parker, a professor in the University of Washington's social studies education department. A wonderful teacher, Walter "translates" research and methods for ordinary classroom teachers in a way that is warm, invitational, and most of all doable. He was speaking on a new topic, biographies and the social studies classroom.

As most after-school inservices do, this one took a few minutes to get started: friends from neighboring schools greeting one another; the usual coffee, tea, and donuts, some politically correct fresh fruit thrown in; administrators doing head counts. Puzzled eyes kept bumping into me. I stared intently at the floor beneath my feet: What does one do when doing nothing? I figured that as long as I hadn't helped myself to any of the goodies, no one would throw me out! Then Walter arrived, escorted by a friend who worked in this large school district and who had told me of Walter's visit. I made brief eye contact and then hunkered down, invisible once again.

After Walter's introduction, I relaxed. He began his theme, and I started taking notes like mad. Once again, he transformed current research and methods, this time through the wisdom of Myra Zarnowski, a professor from Queens College of the City University of New York and the author of *Learning About Biographies: A Reading-and-Writing Approach for Children,* which had been jointly published by the National Council of Teachers of English and the National Council for the Social Studies in 1990.

Walter, high on Myra's method of organizing cooperative biographies, especially liked the way she suggested that teachers approach cooperative biographies and how her suggestions tied in with the national social studies standards. As Walter explained each step, I got more and more excited. I envisioned it happening in my classroom, and it looked terrific!

The Importance of In-Depth Learning

Myra Zarnowski believes in spending a considerable period of time on a single topic, time during which children can investigate, organize, and manipulate stimulating ideas and materials. I agree. I often ignore curriculum outlines, which frequently stress coverage over depth, and spend our classroom moments on a longer exploration of fewer topics. This is developmentally appropriate in the intermediate grades. Our students are certainly ready to invest themselves in studies of substance. Quick overviews with dabs of theory and a stroke of fact here and there frequently bore our students, turning them off learning and confirming their long-held belief that there's really nothing worth learning.

The Value of Manipulating Material

Zarnowski also believes in manipulatives. We are familiar with manipulatives in math or science classes, but few of us think of history as an area in which the manipulation of material is similarly productive. Zarnowski feels that in history, "the manipulation that occurs is largely through language" (xi). Once students collect interviews, artifacts, reports, and other documents, they must then organize that research so it makes sense. Zarnowski states, "Through the process of selecting and grouping evidence, discussing it, and writing about it, children learn history and language skills at the same time." She uses biographies as a way to give students an in-depth learning experience that includes the manipulation of materials and stimulates genuine conversation.

Question: When You Read Your Book, What Do You Like Best?

I like how everyone did lots of research and how we worked together. Everyone had at least got to a second page.—Kevin

I liked when one chapter ended, the next one started off.—Alissa

I liked the book because we had different writing styles. I gave lots of information.—James

The orderly fashion and the formal way of doing it.—Henley

I liked how we worded it, the words we used, and how we wrote it. I also like how we put it in order.—Becky

I like that we all had basically the same style of writing and it fit together perfectly in the end.—Sarah

Biographies and Standards

Biographies have connections with many of the themes that form the framework of the national social studies standards. Students learn about culture, particularly cultures different from their own, from the true stories of people's lives. Students also learn about time, continuity, and change from biographies. Learning how to read and reconstruct the past by walking in someone else's shoes helps our kids develop historical perspective. Studying people, places, and environments helps students move their locus of comprehension from the personal to a broader, more elastic plane.

Incorporating biographies into social studies also helps students understand themselves. Biographies of people whose lives have made a difference or who have overcome great difficulties are a means by which young learners can contemplate and emulate those people. Many children do not have heroes. Many children have never heard "the rest of the story." They see only the result, not the effort or the defeats that happened prior to success.

Biographies enhance the life vision of our kids, just as good binoculars or a fine microscope helps us see more clearly. These enhanced life visions have the power to transform our students' perceptions of themselves and their surroundings by providing a broader context for their lives. Biographies help children relate personal changes to social, cultural, and historical contexts. Biographies make clear the ways family, gender, ethnicity, nationality, and institutional affiliations contribute to personal identity. Biographies allow children to identify and interpret examples of stereotyping, conformity, and altruism. And the cooperative biography gives students an opportunity to practice working independently and cooperatively to accomplish a common goal.

Moving from Ideas to Practice

A few weeks after Walter's presentation, I carved out a month in which to try the cooperative biography in my classroom. I decided to incorporate it into reading workshop, since we would be doing a lot of reading and related writing. I also decided we should study someone of note who lived during the mid-1800s, because our history topic was the Civil War.

Zarnowski recommends teachers consider four questions prior to choosing a subject:

1. Is the subject's life interesting enough to capture and hold the children's attention?
2. Will a study of the subject's life bring children in contact with major issues and events in history?

3. Will children be learning about a historical figure who is unrepresented or inaccurately represented in textbooks and other curriculum materials?
4. Is there enough literature about this subject for the children to read? (12)

It seemed to me that Abraham Lincoln (my students discovered that he never liked the nickname Abe) fit the criteria. He certainly had an interesting life that would hold the children's attention. His life would definitely bring the students into contact with major issues and a major event in history. He is often stereotyped in textbooks. And more kid-accessible literature is written about him than about all the other famous people who lived in the mid-1800s put together.

It also happens that I am pretty passionate about Abraham Lincoln. He wasn't a paper idol; he was an ordinary person who rose to extraordinary challenges using his common sense and his sense of humor. I like him and I think he is worth studying. My enthusiasm is evident when I announce our new study.

First Things First

I begin by giving my students ten days in which to gather information. Kids in the intermediate grades frequently start a project before the teacher has even finished giving the assignment. They are in such a hurry to get it done that they often skip or skimp on the first step—research. Younger kids wait for the teacher to tell them what they need to know; then they write it down and turn it in. Older kids write down the summaries from the backs of books and turn those in. That isn't what I want to have happen.

"Think of this project like a trip. You're going to leave your home and travel to another time and place in America. You're going to stay for only a short while, so you're going to want to bring back lots of artifacts and documents to remind you of what you have seen and done. You'll want to pack your mental luggage with many souvenirs and take careful notes."

The first five days I read aloud daily to my kids from Russell Freedman's *Lincoln: A Photobiography* during reading workshop. I read for a while, then stop and discuss the information with the kids. Then we take notes. I don't know about your kids, but mine have usually taken few notes and the quality of those they have taken borders on horrible. This is therefore a good time to introduce note taking and give the kids some experience with and some options for using this skill. Because my kids' writing speed varies so greatly, I prepare organizational sheets ahead of time. I vary my approach each day, trying to bring in the multiple intelligences.

On the first day I use a very logical-mathematical approach and outline the material I plan to read aloud. I give each student a copy and when we stop for discussion, they fill in details they think are important or interesting. On the second day, I tap the visual-spatial intelligence as the kids and I create a "mind map" from the material presented. I encourage the kids to draw pictures as well as use words. The third day I appeal to the kinesthetic learner as the kids create a *Jeopardy!*-style game board of facts we'll later use for review for a test. On the fourth day we use interpersonal intelligence as kids

Want to Play with My Civil War Review Board?

work in teams of two or three to come up with one set of notes (I make copies for everyone). Finally, the kids use their intrapersonal intelligence to reflect on Lincoln and his life in a journal entry. After the first year I tried cooperative biography, I learned to ask the kids to keep a time line of Lincoln's life, adding to it after each read-aloud session.

The second week, concentrating on content gets easier because the kids are more familiar with note taking and many begin gravitating toward a style that is comfortable for them. I keep reading aloud for a couple of reasons. One, I want all my kids to have access to some of the same information, and reading aloud ensures that all the children hear the same material and have an opportunity to manipulate it to the best of their ability. Two, reading aloud slows down the impulsive kids, the quicker-than-the-speed-of-light kids, forcing them into a more reflective posture, giving them time to think. During this time, I use more picture books than chapter books. I look for books that will illuminate the era, shed light on how people lived, dressed, and organized their lives. I use the social studies time block to show videos and filmstrips of life in the 1800s. By this time in the year we have studied the life of Harriet Tubman, and my kids are aware of the tension between Northern industrialization and Southern plantation farming. They are beginning to develop a vocabulary that includes terms such as *states' rights*, *abolitionist*, and *secession*. They are becoming aware of how technology—that is, the widespread use of the telegraph—helped bring about Lincoln's election.

Widening the Search

During the third week I ask the kids to unearth content independently. I bring in every book I can find about Lincoln and ask the kids to do the same. I continue reading aloud to the kids for about twenty minutes a day. Then the kids have about twenty minutes in which to do individual research and about twenty minutes more in which to take notes and write journal entries about what they have learned. This is an excellent opportunity to take advantage of any available technology. My kids use the Internet, electronic encyclopedias, databases, and CD-ROMs. Some kids bring in information they find using their home computers. I like to end each day by asking kids to share some new piece of information they have discovered or some question they have as a result of their research. These last five minutes of the day are one of those times I'm glad I'm a teacher. There's nothing quite like hearing kids become passionate about a topic they couldn't have cared less about a couple of weeks earlier. When I hear these children recount what they know about Lincoln, react to him as a person, and empathize with how he might have felt, I know we're doing something worthwhile.

Brainstorming and Organizing

Three weeks of notes! It's time to do something with all the information. I start by having my kids brainstorm everything they know about Lincoln's life. They recall a fact or a tidbit, I write it on the board. (This takes a full reading period and lots of board space!) Everyone contributes. Kids go back to their notes to check details, to remind themselves of events. Their combined knowledge is impressive.

This done, we organize the information by category. This is a turning point in the process of writing biographies. The categories shape the organization of the books the kids will soon be writing. I suspect many teachers and their students are most comfortable with a chronological approach: start at the beginning of the person's life and stop at the end. However, Zarnowski encourages teachers to consider alternatives. Her first suggestion is to begin the biography at the peak of a person's career instead of at birth. She lists five steps to follow in doing this: (1) learn about the subject, (2) develop a time line, (3) identify the watershed event, (4) gather relevant information, (5) write the biography. Zarnowski feels that "this strategy focuses the children's attention on developing a position and backing it up with relevant information. The writer argues either that the subject *was* prepared or *was not* prepared for a later role" (54).

In the life-and-times approach, the children struggle to analyze and understand the relationship between a person and the time in which he or she lived. A life-and-times biography requires a thorough documentation of the times as well as the events in the person's life. Graphic organizers such as T-charts, graphs, and time lines that keep track of the events in history as well as the events in the person's life are critical to using this approach successfully.

Finally, Zarnowski suggests fictionalized biography, a mixture of fiction and nonfiction, giving the writer an opportunity to meld creative writing with fact. This style of writing takes discipline: the writer is not free to make up everything but must create a plausible story about what might have happened. Reading competent examples of fictionalized biography is important here. (Zarnowski recommends F. N. Monjo's biographies as models. Each of his books is about a famous American, and the narrator is always a child who knows that person and discusses her or his habits and achievements.)

Most years, my students nevertheless opt for chronological organization. Because I have thirty kids, I help them decide to use five categories, a chapter devoted to each. We begin placing all the brainstormed details into one of these five categories: early life, family life, law and politics, presidential life, and death.

My "To Do" List for Cooperative Biographies

1. Content packing (1 week). I read aloud and kids take notes.
2. Content stacking(1 week). Kids read independently and take notes.
3. Brainstorm key events (1 period). Whole class participates.
4. Categorize events (1 period). Whole class participates.
5. Independent writing (3–5 periods). Each child.
6. Jigsaw into group sharing by chapter (1–3 periods). Small group work.

7. Rewrite and refine (1–2 periods). Individual or small groups.
8. Meet with book group and share (1–2 periods). Small groups.
9. Revise and refine (1–3 periods). Small groups.
10. Add dedication, introduction, table of contents, bibliography, about the authors, rave reviews, and a cover (3–4 periods). Small groups.
11. Publish and distribute (1–2 periods). Small groups.
12. Read and evaluate (1–2 periods). Individual and whole class.

Cooperative Biographers' Workshop

I divide my class into six cooperative groups of five students each. (This means I'll end up with six books about Abraham Lincoln, each book with five chapters, each chapter written by a single group member.) The kids reorganize the room so their desks are close together and they will be able to talk to each other easily and quietly. Their first major task is deciding who is going to write what. Once that decision is made, silence descends on the room. The authors are at work, some at their desks, some at computer terminals, some lying on the floor in the back of the room. Everyone is writing his or her own chapter.

Later in the week, I reconfigure the groups. This is where the cooperation starts. All the kids writing chapter one gather to share their drafts, as do the chapter two folks, the chapter three people, and so on. They critique, support, supplement, and share with each other, a true writers' workshop. After about a week of this same-chapter arrangement, they are ready to share their chapters in their own book group, reading them aloud to one another.

The computer is an enormous help. Students who have word-processed their work can quickly run copies for their group members to read. Editing becomes a "family affair," strengthening the whole group. Most of my groups are usually able to put their work on the word processor. We use the two computers in my classroom and make deals with other teachers down the hall to let us use their classroom computers when the students in that class are doing other things. (One group that chose not to use the computer later said in their evaluation, "We gave up on trying to make it better. It was too hard to rewrite the parts we didn't like.")

The groups always discover that they need to do some rewriting and reshaping to make the chapters fit, adding things that got left out between chapters and deleting things that are repetitive or unimportant. They work hard to get the chapters in the same tense, in the same voice, in a similar style. As one girl said after a particularly intense session with her group, "I never knew words mattered so much!"

Question: What Would You Change?

I would change the fonts to all be the same.—Locke

I would change my chapter. It needed more details.—Laura

If I had more information, I think we could have done better.

—Amy

Nothing. I like my book and I don't want to change it!—Ken

I would type it on the computer.—Alissa

I would like to correct the misspelling of one person's name. I would like to have thanked my grandparents in the dedication. I would have liked to have written more about myself in About the Author.—Aaron

Assessing Cooperative Biographies

One of the major reasons for undertaking a cooperative biography in the classroom is to enable students to apply and integrate interpersonal skills and academic skills authentically. The National Council for the Social Studies divides the essential skills for social studies into three distinct categories: acquiring information, organizing and using information, and interpersonal relationships and social participation. Identifying these skills in a format adapted from *How to Assess Authentic Learning*, by Kay Burke (1994), I constructed the observation checklist from the NCSS list of essential skills, in Appendix 5-1. I use this checklist primarily to encourage my kids to assess their own progress as well as that of the entire group. I find this checklist helpful for improving group performance as well as identifying who needs help cooperating with others.

Cooperation is not learned in a day or in a single unit. Developing this kind of skill frequently takes years, because students are seldom given concrete examples of when they are successful and when they are not. The observation checklist allows a peer, a parent, a teacher, or the child him/herself to check off whether or not the student can demonstrate the skill or behavior being measured. It's a quick, easy way to observe and record those skills we often neglect to assess even though they are critical to the success of the project. Teaching cooperation skills while they're "hot" is much more effective than discussing what might have been after the project is over. Behavior change is more immediate and more likely to be repeated when I observe the unsuccessful behavior, promptly ask the student to identify it, and then ask volunteers to role-play alternative outcomes.

The Finishing Touches

In addition to writing the individual chapters, each group also creates a cover. Most use the computer and cut and paste a combination of print and illustration. They also compose a table of contents and an "about the authors" page. Many add a dedication. They are required to include a bibliography and are encouraged to add an endnote reflecting on what this project has meant to them. Sometimes I ask them to fabricate some one-sentence reviews attributed to figures from popular culture; this adds a bit of fun to the project and allows the kids to demonstrate their sense of humor as well as how much they value their book about Lincoln's life. Lindsay, Aaron, Dan, and Laura included the following reviews.

Some people who have loved this book:

"A spiffy book."—$Richie $ Rich$

"An all righty then book."—Jim Carey

"It makes your hair stand up."—Kramer

"I can't jump higher than this book."—Michael Jordan

Question: How Do You Feel Your Group Worked Together?

The only thing I have doubts about is sometimes our group members wouldn't listen to each other.—Aaron

We were just a good group.—Kevin

We didn't have a single fight.—Katrina

We worked well but it's hard to keep all the papers together.—Mike

Some of us worked well, some of us didn't.—Elizabeth

Sometimes people were disagreeable, but in the long run everyone has to be at one point.—Amy

We all did our share.—Kris

We usually just worked, but sometimes we didn't get along.
—Henley

We all had different ideas, but we combined them.—James

Some people didn't do a lot, but others worked together and did things to help our book.—Dan

Endnote

Cooperative biographies have added depth to my intermediate classroom. Even though we think we have provided ample opportunity, students oftentimes are asked to write about topics of which they know little. Seldom are students given class time to read and research prior to writing. I liken this period to a pool of water. Students who have both time and resources to develop a well of knowledge write deeply as their words flow and their ideas float among facts and thoughtful observations. Students who do not have this time built into their writing assignment are like a bucket brigade trying to scoop water from a mud puddle. They are certain to fail. I would rather do one or two cooperative biographies a year than several reports that only skim the surface of a shallow reservoir of content.

I'm determined never again to ask my students to write without time for reading, research, and thinking. I find my kids feel more successful and they are more successful. No more reports dragged in from home, cut and pasted off Encarta or copied from a library book. No longer do my students' moms get "B's" for their work. We do all of our writing in class. And all of our reading. And all of our research. Thanks, Myra and Walter. You've influenced my classroom profoundly.

Appendix 5-1: Observation Checklist

Student _____ Class _____ Date _____

Type of Assignment _____

_____ Teacher   Date _____   Signed _____

_____ Peer   Date _____   Signed _____

_____ Self   Date _____   Signed _____

	Usually	Sometimes	Not Yet
Finds information:			
• Uses various parts of a book (index, table of contents, etc.)	____	____	____
• Uses key words, encyclopedia volumes, indexes, and cross-references to find information	____	____	____

- Evaluates sources of information (print, films and videotapes, electronic media)   ____   ____   ____
- Selects passages that are about the topic   ____   ____   ____
- Adjusts speed of reading to suit purpose   ____   ____   ____
- Adjusts rate of reading to fit difficulty of material   ____   ____   ____

Arranges information in usable form:
- Makes outline or "mind map" of topic   ____   ____   ____
- Makes time line   ____   ____   ____
- Takes notes   ____   ____   ____
- Keeps records   ____   ____   ____
- Listens for information   ____   ____   ____
- Follows direction   ____   ____   ____
- Prepares a bibliography   ____   ____   ____

Demonstrates group interaction skills:
- Contributes to the development of a supportive group climate   ____   ____   ____
- Participates in making rules and guidelines for group life   ____   ____   ____
- Serves as a leader or a follower   ____   ____   ____
- Assists in setting group goals   ____   ____   ____
- Participates in delegating duties, organizing, planning, making decisions, and taking action in a group setting   ____   ____   ____
- Participates in persuading, compromising, debating, and negotiating in the resolution of conflicts and differences   ____   ____   ____

Comments:

Appendix 5-2: A Cooperative Biography
Written by Five Fifth Graders

The Life Story of Abraham Lincoln by Kelsey A. Florence, Peter J. Goldman, Dana M. Goverman, Molly C. Mulally, and Craig T. Waterhouse

Dedications

Molly dedicates this book to the Whales Foundation.

Craig dedicates this book to the city of Mercer Island.

Peter dedicates this book to Abraham Lincoln and his family. Peter also dedicates this to his own family.

Kelsey dedicates this book to Abraham Lincoln and Bugs Bunny.

Dana dedicates this book to her family.

Table of Contents

Chapter One: Early Life

On February 12, 1809, Nancy Hanks gave birth to a baby boy. Thomas Lincoln, father, and Nancy Hanks named the boy Abraham, for his grandfather. He was born in a one-room cabin in Hodgenville, Kentucky. Most people called him "Abe," but Abraham hated it.

When he was two years old, he moved with his family to Knob Creek Farm. His first teachers were at Knob Creek Farm. The schoolteachers were very strict. Children didn't go to school a lot. They went a couple of weeks a year. The schools were called "blab" school, because the children just shouted out their lessons. Abraham's first teacher was Zachariah Riney. Abraham never forgot him, because he was so strict. Fair, but strict.

He moved again when he was eight years old with his family to Little Pigeon Creek. There he was old enough and strong enough to hold an axe. Dennis Hanks was Abraham's cousin, and he was the first boy that Abraham had ever seen.

Soon, Abraham's mother, Nancy, died of milk sickness. Abraham helped build his mother's coffin out of cherry wood. Thomas went back to Kentucky to find a new wife. He finally married Sarah Bush Johnston, who had three children of her own.

Whenever you saw him, Abraham was always reading a book. He borrowed books and newspapers to read.

When Abraham was seventeen, he left home and went to work as a ferryman's helper. A year later his sister died while giving birth to her first child. So now you know a little bit about Abraham Lincoln's early life.

Chapter Two: Family Life

When Abraham was twenty-one he moved away to New Salem, Illinois, from his family in Indiana. He arrived in July 1831. He got a job chopping wood and other jobs he was good at. Then he got a job at the general store in New Salem. He liked this job because he had lots of time to read because the store wasn't busy. One day Jack Armstrong, the town wrestling champion, challenged Abraham to a match, Abraham won. The general store went out of business.

A war against Chief Black Hawk started. Abraham joined the militia for three months but never sighted any Indians, only mosquitoes.

Abraham decided to start a general store with his friend William Berry. The store soon went belly-up. Then William Berry died and left Abe with $1,100 in debts. He had lots of different jobs but it still took him fifteen years to pay off the debts. He became the postmaster of New Salem. People began to call him Honest Abe, which he hated. He moved to Vandalia, the capital of Illinois, because of his job. Then he had to move to Springfield, which was the new capital of Illinois. Abraham was lonely.

After living in Springfield for a short while, Abraham was trying to get out of a current romance with Mary Owens. Abraham was rejected. Soon Abraham met Mary Todd and knew he shouldn't marry her, yet he couldn't withstand her. But on January 7, 1841, Abraham broke the engagement with Mary Todd. On November 4, 1842, Abe and Mary Todd were married. Nine months later, their first son, Robert, was born in 1843. Then Eddie was born in 1846. Then Willie was born in 1850. Abraham liked him the most. Eddie died in Springfield at the age of four. But soon after that, the last child, Tad, was born in 1853. In 1862, Willie died at the White House at age eleven. Then Tad died in Chicago. Soon after Lincoln's assassination, Mary Todd went insane because of all the deaths, and her son Robert put her in a mental institute for a couple of months.

Chapter Three: Law and Political Life
Abraham Lincoln was a very happy man when it came to his law and political life. He started out by borrowing law books from John T. Stuart, his future law partner. He studied them for two years and then was ready. When he moved from New Salem to Springfield, he rode into town on a borrowed horse and had $7 in his pocket. He was a junior partner to Stuart and slept on a couch in their law office.

Then he met Joshua Speed, who offered to share a room above his general store. Speed's store was a kind of meeting place for men to come and swap stories and argue politics. One of those men was Stephen R. Douglas.

Once he and Lincoln started talking, they both knew that they were rivals. Lincoln was a Whig and Douglas, a Democrat. The Whigs were a group that soon died down and became Republicans. Lincoln wanted to get ahead of Douglas a lot.

In law his partner taught him how to talk in court because all he knew was what was in the books. Soon Lincoln and Stuart were very busy. In politics he rose in the Whig party and got reelected to legislature four times. He also started coaching Young Whigs. Douglas was also coaching Young Democrats. After about five years, he started his own law office and invited a young man to be his junior partner. That man was William Herndon.

Back to politics. Lincoln got elected to a seat in the House of Representatives in 1846. He took his wife, Mary, and their two sons, Robert and Eddie, to Washington. But soon Mary decided that she was bored and unhappy in Washington D.C. After three months, she stuffed her suitcase and she, plus the two boys, moved in with her family until Lincoln's term was over. He constantly wrote to them so they wouldn't forget him. After his term, which was a disappointment, the Whigs tried to get him out in a nice way. It worked. Now Lincoln was out of politics for the time. He was a full-time lawyer. But the worst wasn't over yet. Eddie, their second son, grew very ill for two months, then died. Mary shut herself in her room for weeks and Lincoln buried himself in his work.

Lincoln and Herndon, his partner, both didn't care about neatness so you could find orange seeds sprouting in dusty corners of the office. But they were neat enough to handle one hundred cases a year. Lincoln was now one of the most sought-after attorneys in the state and mastered every detail before going to court. He was a very good lawyer and always addressed the court with wit and humor. When he was picking a jury he would try to pick fat men because he believed they were jolly and easily swayed. He could also translate the most complicated sentence into the simplest terms.

Chapter Four: Presidential Life

On November 6, 1860, fifty-one-year-old Abraham Lincoln was elected president. Lincoln had 1,865,593 votes, Douglas had 1,382,713 votes, and Breckinridge had 848,356 votes. A young girl named Grace Bedell suggested that Abraham should grow a beard and he did.

March 4, 1861: Lincoln took the oath of office that day in front of the unfinished U.S. Capitol. Washington looked like an armed camp. All morning the cavalry and artillery had been clattering through the streets. Troops were scattered everywhere. There were rumors of assassination plots. The southern plans were to seize the capital and prevent the inauguration. That had put the army on alert. Lincoln was nervous. He wore a black suit and held a silk stovepipe hat in one hand. Lincoln was a six-foot-four-inch, 180-pound, black-haired, absentminded, high-pitched-voiced man who told jokes or anecdotes to people when they called or visited him.

Lincoln, who was the tallest president, ranks as one of the greatest leaders in American history. He was the first U.S. president born outside of the thirteen original colonies. The schooling he had added all together was a little more than one year. The rest of it he thought himself. He was a most eloquent speaker. Also he was the finest writer of all the presidents. A couple of names that people called him were Savior of the Union and the Great Emancipator. Lincoln, who was against slavery since he was a little boy and saw a slave auction, signed the Emancipation Proclamation in 1862 that freed all the slaves. They were to be freed on January 1, 1863, in Arkansas, Texas, Louisiana, Mississippi, Alabama, Florida, Georgia, South Carolina, North Carolina, and Virginia.

The Civil War started right after Lincoln became president. When Abraham and Mary moved into the White House, they moved in with their two sons, Tad and Willie. One year later Willie died. Lincoln went to Gettysburg and made a speech called the Gettysburg Address. The part of the Gettysburg Address that most people know by heart is "Fourscore and seven years ago our forefathers brought forth on this continent a new nation, conceived in liberty, and dedicated to the proposition that all men are created equal." The Civil War ended April 9, 1865.

The secret to all his success was his character—honesty, love, justice, kindness, perseverance, humor, and according to Lincoln, "the providence of God."

Chapter Five: Death and What His Life Means to Us

Mr. Lincoln had a nightmare that he was walking in the White House and he heard people weeping. He was looking everywhere, but he couldn't find them. Finally, he entered a large room, the East

Room. He saw a coffin with a body that was wrapped up inside. There was a stillness in the room and he asked, "Who's dead in the White House?" A Union soldier answered, "The president. He was killed by an assassin." Then he woke up. Mr. Lincoln was very troubled by his dream.

Mr. Lincoln went with Mary Todd to see a play at Ford's Theater in Washington, D.C. That play was called "Our American Cousin." The lead role was played by Laura Keene. She had played the role one thousand times. It was written by Tom Taylor. John F. Parker was supposed to be guarding the president's box, but turned out to be unreliable. He couldn't see the play so he went and sat in the dress circle. The box was unprotected when John W. Booth crept in. There is some confusion about Abraham Lincoln's last words. Some think they were, "How I should like to visit Jerusalem sometime," while others believe Mrs. Lincoln said, "What will Mrs. Harris think of me hanging on you so?" and Mr. Lincoln replied, "She won't think anything about it."

John Wilkes Booth was a young, handsome man with a mustache. He stopped to pick up his mail at Ford's Theater because he was an actor there and he used it as his mailing address. While he was there, he heard that President Lincoln would be attending the play that night. He thought that this would be a perfect time to carry out his plans and try to kill Lincoln as well as Vice-President Johnson and Secretary of State Seward. Booth was an actor from the South and he hated Lincoln. About 10:15 on April 14, he walked to the president's box. He drew his single-shot, muzzle-loading derringer, .44 caliber. When Booth fired, the bullet pierced Lincoln's skull near his left ear and stopped behind the right eye. The president slumped down in his seat and Mrs. Lincoln screamed out in horror.

When the Civil War ended, most northerners wanted to treat the southerners badly. Lincoln's reaction was that they should treat them as brothers. He said "With malice toward none and charity for all." This made some people mad. He had a lot of enemies.

The president was carried across the street and put on a bed. He was too big for it so they laid him diagonally. There were lots of doctors trying to save Lincoln, but on April 15, 1865, President Lincoln was dead. He died at an age of fifty-six. He was buried next to his son Willie.

Lewis Paine and some others failed to kill Seward. The people who were supposed to kill Johnson got too scared and didn't even try. Most of them were arrested shortly after. After her husband's death, Mary Todd Lincoln became mentally unstable. She had to live like a homeless person with no money and a bad home for three years because Mr. Lincoln died without a will. The judge didn't like Mary, so it took a long time to get her fair share of money.

Mr. Lincoln's life means a lot to us today. It might have taken us a long time to get rid of slavery if we hadn't had Mr. Lincoln as a president. The war could have lasted longer and cost our country more money. Abraham Lincoln was a very important person in United States history because he was a good leader and a wonderful person. He kept the union from splitting into two different countries and that would have severely cut the economy. Without Lincoln our country could be a very different place.

Bibliography

Encarta Encyclopedia. 1996. Microsoft: Bellevue, WA.

FREEDMAN, RUSSELL. 1987. *Lincoln: A Photobiography.* Clarion Books: New York.

GROSS, RUTH B. 1973. *True Stories About Abraham Lincoln.* Scholastic Inc.: New York.

HAYMAN, LEROY. 1968. *The Death of Lincoln.* Scholastic Inc.: New York.

LAWLISS, CHUCK. 1991. *The Civil War Source Book.* Harmony Books: New York.

MCGOVERN, ANN. 1992. *If You Grew Up with Abraham Lincoln.* Scholastic Inc.: New York.

About the Authors

Kelsey enjoys riding horses and playing soccer in her spare time. She also likes to ride jet skis. She wrote the presidential life chapter.

Peter likes to play football and baseball in his spare time. He has a dog, two cats, a bird, and also fish. He wrote the chapter on law and political life.

Dana plays soccer and reads. She has two cats, a hamster, and a tank full of fish (too many to count). She wrote the chapter on death.

Molly enjoys playing soccer and dancing. She also plays on the computer in her spare time. She wrote the chapter on early life.

Craig likes to play football, basketball, and soccer. He has one pixie bobcat. He wrote the chapter on family life.

Reviews

The best book ever written, and I'm not kidding! !—Gumby

Way cool, man!!!—Bart Simpson

Excellent! ! !—Bill and Ted

As fun to read as eating a carrot!!!—Bugs Bunny

♀✉✳◆☺♀☀♂⊕↕♋!!♱—Aliens from planet Zorb

Bibliography for Cooperative Biography, Slavery, Lincoln, and the Civil War

ACKERMAN, KAREN. 1990. *The Tin Heart*. New York: Atheneum. A picture book that effectively portrays the toll the Civil War took on friends.

ALTMAN, SUSAN, and SUSAN LECHNER. 1993. *Followers of the North Star*. Chicago: Children's Press. Wonderful, informative poetry about African American heroes, heroines, and historical times.

BEATTY, PATRICIA. 1987. *Charley Skedaddle*. New York: Troll. An easy-to-read winner of the Scott O'Dell Award for Historical Fiction, this story illustrates that "courage is in the eye of the beholder."

The Blue and the Grey (videotape). 1982. Columbia Tristar Home Video (295 min.). This five-hour docudrama about the Civil War helps students get a visual handle on how people lived during the mid-1800s and introduces most of the issues dealt with in Civil War studies for this age group. I show an hour each day for a week and think it is worth the time. Some communities may object to some of the language; teacher preview is recommended.

BRADBY, MARIE. 1995. *More than Anything Else.* New York: Orchard. Beautiful, powerful picture book about Booker T. Washington's childhood. This one should be read to children whether they are studying the Civil War or not.

BUNTING, EVE. 1996. *The Blue and the Grey.* New York: Scholastic. Unique picture book contrasting the misery and destruction of the Civil War with the construction of a modern interracial community.

CLARK, MARGARET GOFF. 1980. *Freedom Crossing.* New York: Scholastic. Laura discovers her brother and father are helping slaves escape into Canada. She believes helping a fugitive slave is breaking the law. Then she meets Martin Paige, a twelve-year-old runaway slave who would rather die than be sent back to the South.

COLLIER, JAMES LINCOLN, and CHRISTOPHER COLLIER. 1997. *With Every Drop of Blood.* New York: Dell. Two young men, one a reb and the other a black Yankee, form an unlikely alliance in the final days of the Civil War.

EVERETT, GWEN. 1993. *John Brown: One Man Against Slavery.* New York: Rizzoli. Stunning visual presentation of Jacob Lawrence's paintings accompanied by a unique perspective on John Brown, that of his youngest daughter, Annie.

FLEISCHMAN, PAUL. 1993. *Bull Run.* New York: HarperCollins. Compelling collection of sixteen different points of view drawn from actual accounts by the people who were there and experienced the true nature of war. Easy to read, this book has all the ingredients for readers' theater.

FREEDMAN, RUSSELL. 1987. *Lincoln: A Photobiography.* New York: Clarion. Can be read aloud or read alone. Excellent resource for overview of Lincoln's life. Photographs are particularly informative and personal.

FRITZ, JEAN. 1987. *Brady.* New York: Puffin. Brady suspects neighbors are assisting runaway slaves. He finds out it's much closer to home when he learns of his father's part in the slavery controversy. Brady can't keep a secret and that gets him into big trouble

———. 1993. *Just a Few Words, Mr. Lincoln: The Story of the Gettysburg Address.* New York: Grosset & Dunlap. Very easy reading. Great basic information for all.

GAUCH, PATRICIA LEE. 1975. *Thunder at Gettysburg*. New York: Bantam Doubleday Dell. Extremely quick and easy read packed with information. It's based on Lincoln's autobiographical account and can be used in tandem with Lincoln and McCurdy's *Gettysburg Address*.

GROSS, RUTH BELOV. 1973. *True Stories About Abraham Lincoln*. New York: Scholastic. Lincoln comes alive for the least capable readers in this paperback containing twenty-two short, easy-to-read stories about our sixteenth president.

GROSSMAN, JULIAN. 1991. *The Civil War: Battlefields and Campgrounds in the Art of Winslow Homer*. New York: Abradale Press. Outstanding art book with annotations. Helps us all understand not only what was happening but how it was interpreted by an artist of the time.

HAYMAN, LEROY. 1968. *The Death of Lincoln: A Picture History of the Assassination*. New York: Scholastic. Challenging and detailed, this biography of Lincoln's final hours and what happened after he died reveals facts and information children never get from history textbooks. More than fifty photos, drawings, and paintings from the time further illuminate the tragic true story of Lincoln's death.

HOPKINSON, DEBORAH. 1993. *Sweet Clara and the Freedom Quilt*. New York: Knopf. Based on a true story in African American history, this read-aloud book celebrates a young girl's resourcefulness and courage. Excellent companion to books about Harriet Tubman.

HUMES, JAMES C. 1996. *The Wit and Wisdom of Abraham Lincoln*. New York: HarperCollins. Lincoln's humor and wisdom is transmitted to young historians via more than a thousand quotations and anecdotes, listed alphabetically by topic. A most complete time line is included.

KALMAN, BOBBIE. 1993. *Historic Communities: 19th Century Clothing*. New York: Crabtree. Depicting everything from footwear and underwear to hair styles and hats, this paperback provides excellent visual clues to the life and times of folks living in the mid-1800s.

LAWRENCE, JACOB. 1993. *Harriet and the Promised Land*. New York: Simon & Schuster. Paintings by Jacob Lawrence. Wonderful read-aloud companion to other books about Harriet Tubman.

LESTER, JULIUS. 1968. *To Be a Slave*. New York: Dial. Excerpts from this book make excellent reading for individual students or as a read-aloud to the class.

LEVINE, ELLEN. 1993. *If You Traveled on the Underground Railroad*. New York:

Scholastic. Excellent resource for quickly getting all your students "on board" regarding the Underground Railroad.

LINCOLN, ABRAHAM, illustrated by Michael McCurdy. 1995. *The Gettysburg Address*. Boston: Houghton Mifflin. Fantastic illustrations. Can be used in connection with copies of Lincoln's drafts of the address in his own handwriting, which are available on the Internet at http://lcweb.loc.gov/exhibits/G.Address/gadrft.html. Can also be used in connection with Gauch's short and informative book.

LUCAS, ALICE. 1991. *Twelve Years a Slave* (three audiocassettes and a teacher's guide). Available from Many Cultures Publishing, P.O. Box 425646, San Francisco, CA 94142-5646, 1-800-484-4173 ext. 1073, fax 415-626-7276. (Materials on immigration are available as well.) Outstanding oral reading of first-person account of an African American who was kidnapped and sold into slavery. Some music included.

LUNN, JANET. 1981. *The Root Cellar*. London: Puffin. This book appeals to competent readers and is best read after having studied the Civil War.

MCGOVERN, ANN. 1966. *If You Grew Up with Abraham Lincoln*. New York: Scholastic. Thirty questions kids typically ask about Lincoln and the times he grew up in are answered in this student-friendly paperback.

MCKISSACK, PATRICIA C., and FREDRICK L. MCKISSACK. 1994. *Christmas in the Big House, Christmas in the Quarters*. New York: Scholastic. Excellent picture book comparing life in the master's home to life in the slave quarters. Well researched. A book for all seasons!

MELTZER, MILTON, ed. 1989. *Voices from the Civil War: A Documentary History of the Great American Conflict*. New York: HarperCollins. Works well for a teacher to read aloud or as a source for readings for individual students. These point-of-view pieces are taken from primary sources.

MOORE, KAY. 1994. *If You Lived at the Time of the Civil War*. New York: Scholastic. Presented in easily read question-and-answer format, this book contrasts life in the South with life in the North. Recommended introduction to differing points of view.

MURPHY, JIM. 1990. *The Boys' War*. Boston: Houghton Mifflin. A book of eye-opening photos accompanied by readable text. Told from the point of view of both Union and Confederate soldiers. Excellent background for Polacco's *Pink and Say*.

NORTHRUP, SOLOMON. 1968. *Twelve Years a Slave*. New Orleans: Louisiana State University Press. See audiotape description on previous page, under Lucas, Alice.

POLACCO, PATRICIA. 1994. *Pink and Say*. New York: Philomel. One of the most effective picture books about war and humanity I have ever read. A must!

PRICE, WILLIAM H. 1961. *Civil War Handbook*. Fairfax, VA: L. B. Prince. Chock-full of little-known but important facts, ranging from a list of "firsts" the Civil War ushered in, such as "first practical machine gun, first large-scale use of land mines, first multimanned submarine, first photograph taken in combat," to pictures of camp life and comparisons of uniforms. A chronology of battles and a map of major battlefields is included.

REEDER, CAROLYN. 1989. *Shades of Gray*. New York: Simon & Schuster. Orphaned by the Civil War, Will was forced to live with his Uncle Jed, a coward who had refused to fight in the war, a traitor to the Confederacy. Provides a point of view different from both the Union and Confederate sides.

REIT, SEYMOUR. 1988. *Behind Rebel Lines: The Incredible Story of Emma Edmonds, Civil War Spy*. New York: Harcourt Brace. Re-created from memoirs, U.S. Army records, and files from the National Archives, this is a story of an incredible spy who answered Lincoln's plea for volunteers. Well written for intermediate-grade readers.

RINGGOLD, FAITH. 1992. *Aunt Harriet's Underground Railroad in the Sky*. New York: Crown. A great wrap-up read-aloud. It revisits many of the concepts discussed during Civil War studies.

RUBY, LOIS. 1994. *Steal Away Home*. New York: Macmillan. History, drama, and mystery are interwoven in two overlapping stories: one of the Underground Railroad in the 1850s and the other of a curious young girl in Lawrence, Kansas, in the 1990s.

SHORTO, RUSSELL. 1991. *Abraham Lincoln and the End of Slavery*. Brookfield, CT: Millbrook Press. This thirty-two-page paperback succinctly encapsulates this phase of American history in a highly readable fashion.

STEELE, WILLIAM O. 1986. *The Perilous Road*. San Diego: Harcourt Brace. Basically a Confederate point of view. Many children need help with the dialect until they get comfortable reading this interesting story.

STERLING, DOROTHY. 1954. *Freedom Train: The Story of Harriet Tubman*. New York: Scholastic. An outstanding biography. I have all my students read this one.

TURNER, ANN. 1987. *Nettie's Trip South*. New York: Simon & Schuster. A read-aloud picture book that presents a Northern child's point of view regarding slavery.

TURNER, GLENNETTE TILLEY. 1989. *Take a Walk in Their Shoes*. New York: Dutton. Biographies of fourteen African Americans in play format. Excellent for readers' theater or shadow puppets.

WINTER, JEANETTE. 1992. *Follow the Drinking Gourd*. New York: Knopf. A read-aloud picture book. Great introduction to the Underground Railroad.

ZARNOWSKI, MYRA. 1990. *Learning About Biographies: A Reading-and-Writing Approach for Children*. Urbana, IL: National Council for Teachers of English and National Council for the Social Studies. Available by calling 800-369-6283. This practical book is divided into two parts. Part 1 provides background information about the nature of biography and the biographer's task. Part 2 describes four strategies for using biography in the classroom. Great resource for teachers who want to begin their own biography-centered programs.

SIX

Bridges to Other Cultures: Infusing Cultural Studies Across the Curriculum

> Social studies programs should include experiences that provide for the study of culture and cultural diversity.
>
> —NCSS Standard

I can't imagine teaching and not using strategies from diverse cultures to help my kids learn. Even if a person doesn't teach social studies, bringing in cultural arts, patterns, and ideas enlivens the classroom and promotes an aura of understanding that lasts. Taking part in a Chinese shadow puppet play, creating a set of Japanese story cards, or playing an Inuit game in the classroom arouses a receptiveness to the new or the different. When students discuss activities like these from a cultural perspective, they often find common or familiar characteristics.

Continued contact with diverse cultures encourages students to relate positively to others, both nationally and globally. Even a single cultural experience in the classroom can trigger a lifelong interest in a country and its people or a personal insight about self and others. Integrating cultural activities into the regular school day taps student interest in individuals and societies different from themselves and paves avenues for understanding different points of view. Students who experience other cultures often learn as much about themselves as they do about others.

Starting with Stories

Any teacher can add a cultural dimension to his or her classroom by choosing to read literature from other cultures. Whether it is a picture book or a novel, children learn from the teacher's very choice what's okay and what's not. If all the children hear are stories about one ethnic group, then it's not unlikely they will get the message that one and only one group is okay. Sharing the wealth of cultural stories enriches everyone. Certainly common values, shared desires, and, yes, even universal follies deserve a spot in our school schedules. Humor from around the world or sensitivity to concerns within the community can be shared through the power of story.

Folktales are generally defined as prose narratives that are passed down through the generations orally. They are usually timeless, are not based on historical events or set in a historical place, and are not really meant to be believed as either historical or religious truth. Because they are told, not written, there are usually many versions. (When one version becomes better known than the others, it's primarily because someone somewhere finally writes it down.)

Jacob and Wilhelm Grimm recorded many European folktales in the nineteenth century. Wolfram Eberhard collected and analyzed thousands of Chinese folktales. Some, such as the story of Cinderella, appear in both Western and Chinese versions. The Chinese Cinderella, Yeh Shen, dates from the Tang dynasty (A.D. 618–907), while the earliest known Western version is one popular in Italy in 1634. There are over seven hundred versions of Cinderella, from countries as diverse as Egypt, Ireland, France, India, Nigeria, and Zimbabwe. Different Native American nations—the Zuni and the Algonquin, for example—also have their Cinderella stories. Teachers enjoy sharing these tales with their students. Tricksters, three wishes, and royalty in disguise are other themes that can be traced around the globe.

I often replace reading workshop with shadow theater for a week, integrating this cultural art form with our study of immigration in social studies. I start with a Chinese folktale, "Three Precious Pearls," to which I then add shadow puppets. Studying this Chinese folktale helps my students identify the universality of many of the values they hold. Using the shadow puppets personalizes this knowledge.

A Brief History of Shadow Puppets

A fine teacher's resource entitled *China Mosaic: Multidisciplinary Units for the Middle Grades* (Hammond-Bernson 1988), informs us that, according to legend, shadow puppet theater began in China in 121 B.C. when Wu Di, an emperor of the Han dynasty, was grieving over the death of his favorite concubine. A Taoist priest used shadow to evoke a likeness of the woman in an attempt to alleviate his ruler's sorrow. The shadow was so lifelike that the Emperor thought his love lived once more.

Shadows exist in the magical world between reality and dreams. In many cultures, shadows are a link with spirits or the dead or are a part of ritual. Shadow puppetry is common in many parts of Asia, but it is in China where shadow play probably had its start.

This teacher's resource notes shadow-puppet shows became popular during the Song dynasty (A.D. 960–1279). Itinerant storytellers used shadow to illustrate stories of warfare, romance, chivalry, or Buddhist legend. On special occasions, the storytellers were invited into private homes or to the emperor's court. This form of entertainment was especially welcomed by women. Because women were not allowed to attend the theater, the shadow play was one of their few experiences with the sort of entertainment men witnessed at the opera.

A puppet troupe was often a family whose members were the puppeteers, musicians, and singers. These troupes would travel from village to village. The musical accompaniment and sound effects created by both string and percussion instruments highlighted the action of the play.

The puppets, according to *China Mosaic*, were made from animal or fish skins, donkey skin being the most durable. A master puppeteer might have more than one hundred figures and a thousand interchangeable heads. An individual puppet might consist of as many as ten separate pieces. Holes or slits were artfully cut in the puppets to let light pass through. They were brightly colored, and this color would be visible through the mulberry bark screen.

China Mosaic concludes that, traditionally, shadow theater has been part entertainment, part instruction. Most of the stories that delighted audiences for centuries imparted a moral as well. Shadow theater has continued to be used by the Chinese government in its dealings with rural people.

Shadow Puppets in the Classroom: A Diary

Day 1

We needed a change of pace. The kids had been reading, writing, and discussing chapter books for weeks, it seemed. They needed to be more active. My reluctant readers were ready to rebel. I needed a strategy that combines reading with other communication skills and gets the kids out of their chairs, working with each other.

So I introduced the Chinese folktale "The Three Precious Pearls" to the class today. It is a classic tale, recounting the adventures of Shi Wa, a poor young man who must overcome great difficulties to attain a desired goal. He wants to become an apprentice to a master stone-cutter. However, before the stonecutter will take him on, he must obtain three precious pearls from a wise old man in a place far, far away. Undaunted, the youth begins his travels. The first obstacle he encounters is a roaring river. Unable to cross by himself, Shi Wa enlists the aid of a golden dragon. Safely across the river, Shi Wa promises to ask the wise old man when the dragon will be able to summon the wind and rain in the sky.

Next, Shi Wa comes to a towering mountain with no slopes. A phoenix offers to carry him over the mountain. When Shi Wa reaches the other side, the phoenix mentions that she'd like to know when she will be able to mount the clouds and ride the mist. The youth promises to ask the wise old man.

Again proceeding on his way, Shi Wa encounters a sea of flames. A unicorn agrees to carry the boy through the fire. Afterward the

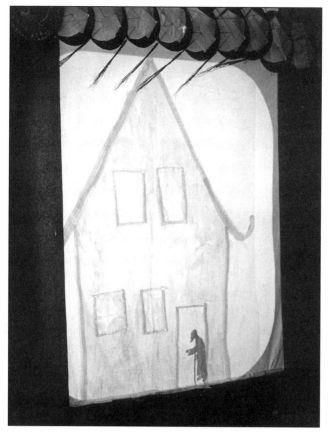

The Master Stonecutter Waits for an Apprentice

unicorn asks Shi Wa to find out from the wise old man why it is possible for the creature to walk through fire but not be able to walk on the road. The boy promises to inquire.

At last Shi Wa, with blistered feet, finds the pine forest where the wise old man resides. Shi Wa is about to ask his questions when the old man cautions, "You can only ask three questions." Shi Wa thinks, What should I do? I have four questions: one for the golden dragon, one for the phoenix, one for the unicorn, and one of my own. If I do not ask for the three pearls, I will not become the stonecutter's apprentice. But I promised my friends the dragon, the phoenix, and the unicorn. I must ask their questions.

On the trip back, Shi Wa first meets the unicorn. "The wise old man said that there is something caught in your right sole. If it is removed, you can walk on the road and feel no pain." The unicorn removes a red stone from his foot and gives it to the boy as a souvenir.

Next Shi Wa reencounters the phoenix. "The wise old man said there is a crippling sore on your tail. If you open it you can mount the clouds and ride the mist." The phoenix removes a yellow stone that is festering on her tail and gives the stone to Shi Wa as a souvenir.

Finally, Shi Wa sees the golden dragon again. "The wise old man said that there is a bone caught in your throat. If you cough it out, you can summon the wind and the rain in the sky." In a couple of coughs, a bone appears, which turns into a white stone. The golden dragon gives Shi Wa the stone as a souvenir.

When the boy returns to the master stonecutter, he is apologetic. Instead of three precious pearls, he gives the stonecutter the three stones and turns to leave. Halted by the master, Shi Wa watches as the stonecutter deftly splits each stone to reveal a precious pearl.

"You thought of others first," says the stonecutter. You were not afraid of hardships. Only in this way can you master skills and become a worthy person. You are the very apprentice I want."

We discussed the story, analyzing the key elements of plot, conflict, and resolution. We examined the moral of the story and discussed how effective it was in teaching behavior valued by the Chinese culture. We discovered that the values highlighted by the story are universal. Then we retold the story, changing the time to the present and the setting to our community. The kids decided it was a good hope-and-wisdom story, one of those stories we read because it teaches us something important or reaches us emotionally.

At the end of the period, I showed shadow puppets to the kids, samples I have collected from former students as well as a couple of authentic ones from China. I suggested that we might create shadow puppets and do plays for our kindergarten buddies, who are studying Chinese New Year customs. If enthusiasm is any predictor of success, we're in for a two-thumbs-up experience!

Day 2

The kids and I began our readers' workshop by discussing what challenges they face as they present the story of "The Three Precious Pearls" using shadow puppets. It's stunning to think that this art form has been popular in China for nearly two thousand years!

The kids are so sharp. They recognized that the audience will not see facial expressions and that the range of movement is limited. To compensate for these handicaps, the kids decided they'd have to use very expressive voices, that the puppet who is "talking" should move in some way, and that they might add music or sound effects.

Sometimes things work out perfectly. This play has six characters, and there are thirty kids in my room. I decided that we would have five performances of the same play. I thought about looking for several other folktales but decided it would be more interesting to see how different groups interpret the same story. Since this was the first dramatic experience of the year, I wrote a script and told the kids that it was available. Each group can decide whether they want to use it as is, alter it a little, or write their own.

We divided into groups by lottery, making sure there were boys and girls in each group. The kids decided who would play what part and got to work, reading their parts aloud.

I gave each student a twelve-inch-square piece of manila tag board. We decided that all the people puppets should be about twelve inches tall, with the animals proportionate to that measure. I provided models of each puppet that the kids could copy if they wanted; they could also create their own. We did decide to limit the number of moving parts to one: the puppeteers of old served long apprenticeships before they were allowed to manipulate more than one part.

I gathered all the paper punches I had and borrowed some from other classrooms so the kids could punch designs into their puppets. They also colored them with bright markers, because surprisingly, this affects the color of the shadows. We used our chopsticks from World Day of Hunger, affixed by a few pieces of transparent tape, to manipulate the puppets. A brad works well to connect the moving part to the body of the figure. The kids spent their readers' workshop

Alyssa and Jenni Practice with Their Puppets

creating their puppets and practicing their lines. Everyone is certainly involved!

Day 3

I got to school early so I could set up the shadow puppet theater before the kids arrived. A white sheet suspended from the ceiling makes a great screen. I stood on student desks, lifted several acoustical tiles out of their metal frames, and tied two ends of the sheet around the metal strips. The main thing is to keep the sheet wrinkle free by making it as taut as possible at the top. I let the bottom of the sheet hang free.

The other requirement is a light source. I used to use clip-on light fixtures, but one day I had a brainstorm: an overhead projector is perfect! By adjusting the distance between the sheet and the projector, the kids can make the image area larger or smaller. I let the kids discover that the overhead goes behind the screen, not in front. They also found they could make the bottom level of the image area high enough so that they can work the puppets kneeling comfortably on the floor by adjusting the overhead.

Each group had time to practice working with the screen and projector. They soon found they needed a coach to tell them how they were doing, since they're behind the screen, not in front of it. Kids from other groups volunteered, happily informing their peers if they talked too softly, didn't move their puppets enough, or rushed through a scene. We taped the script to the sheet. Placing the script so that the kids have to look up to read it helps them project more

Shadow Puppets from the Front

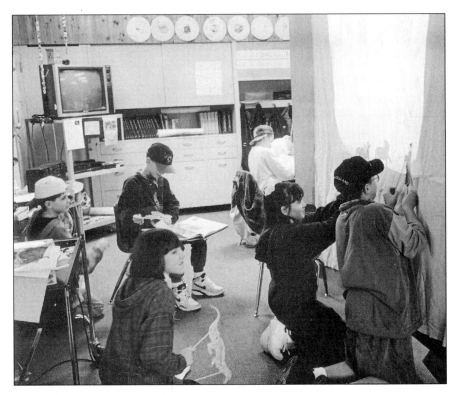

The Same Scene, Backstage

clearly and loudly. Tape recording the script means never having to look down.

The kids who weren't rehearsing worked on scenery. Drawing on overhead transparencies with permanent markers created fabulous backdrops in brilliant colors. The great roaring river, the towering mountain, and the sea of flames came to life on the overhead. Because we had learned that puppeteers in China rest their puppets lightly on the screens in order to create the most effective shadows, the kids practiced gently resting their puppets against the white sheet.

During our readers' workshop today, each group got two rehearsals behind the screen and rehearsed informally several more times. It was a productive day. The kids worked cooperatively and the coaches provided the feedback each group needs to improve. I noticed that several of the kids picked up the copies of Lawrence Yep's books of Chinese folktales that I left around the room. Maybe I'll add a math connection tomorrow and have the kids experiment with tangrams after reading them *Grandfather Tang's Story* (Tompert 1990).

Day 4

Today we held a "coaches' clinic." We all became coaches and watched each group present their play. Everyone said what he or she liked or thought was effective and offered suggestions for improvement. Then each group ran through their play again to try adjustments and find out what the coaches thought about them.

Each group added an introduction of the puppet masters and their puppets. We discussed adding sound effects and music and decided we didn't want to take the time to do that. Instead, we'll play a tape of Chinese music before and after each play.

The kids also decided to make their screen a little fancier. First they hung red butcher paper on either side and across the bottom, vividly framing their "stage." Then they looked up the Chinese characters for fire, wood, water, mountain, loyalty, and perseverance, traced the characters on black paper, cut them out, and attached them to the red paper. Their final touch was to take a Chinese kite I had brought in and string it across the top of the stage to hide the less than elegant job I had done attaching the sheet to the ceiling.

A couple of the kids took to the halls and invited four kindergarten classes and a first grade. Each cast will have a fresh audience. The kids are excited. So am I!

Day 5

Imagine a darkened classroom. The notes of a Chinese symphony float through the air. A group of kindergarten kids are escorted by their fifth-grade buddies to seats in front of a large screen. Without much fuss, the puppet theater lights up and the first shadowed figure begins to speak. The play has begun!

This same scene was played out with four new play casts and four new audiences. At the end of each play, the puppet masters introduced themselves and their puppets. They answered questions from the audience, demystifying the process.

When the plays were over and the audiences gone, we spent some time discussing the experience as a group. Then, as homework, I asked each student to complete a graphic organizer, folded to form a Chinese screen. (See Appendix 6-1 for explanation.)

Shadows, Science, and Civics

I've used the shadow puppet strategy in other contexts as well. Through a series of extraordinary circumstances, my husband and I have spent a week during each of the last three summers in the rain forest of Belize, in Central America, working with Mayan teachers. Many of these teachers have had only one year of teacher training, and some have not completed high school themselves. The schools are primarily state-supported church schools with a national cur-

Brainstorming a PMI Reflection on Shadow Puppets

riculum. Common tools such as overheads, copy machines, and typewriters are practically nonexistent. I've never seen a computer there.

Each morning during the week we work with these teachers, we take field trips to different parts of the community to stimulate the practice of using the community as a classroom. It's fascinating. One day we visit the community development office to learn what is being done to protect the native wildlife as more and more rain forest is being cut down for farms and hydroelectric dams. Another day we climb around a recently excavated Mayan town, complete with temples, or paddle up a river in canoes to visit a Mayan healer and take a walk with her, learning about the medicinal uses of the plants in the rain forest. We visit a contemporary Mayan village where they are trying to revive pottery as an art form, dig our own clay, and try our own hand at it. While Belize may be poor in the tools of today's teaching, it is rich in history and is working hard to shape a future that includes all its diverse citizens and protects its unique plant and animal life.

Last summer, after visiting the community development office, the Mayan teachers discussed the costs and benefits of development in their community. Certainly, electricity is desirable. Until recently, few homes had access to electrical power. Electricity was generated using imported oil and was pretty much limited to the capital, Belize City. Harnessing the rivers for hydroelectricity has proven feasible, but the cost in terms of lost species and flooded ruins is perhaps too high. However, the critical teaching point is that Belizian citizens have a choice. A Chinese shadow-puppet play proved to be a perfect strategy by which these rural teachers could inform the members of their community about the issues.

The teachers wrote a play depicting indigenous animals' view of development: one by one the animals told how they would be affected if they lost their habitat. We then created puppets out of cereal-box cardboard. Bamboo sticks held the puppets up, and the movable parts were tied together with string. We hung a white sheet from the rafters of a classroom. Since they didn't have an overhead projector, flashlights were used to create the shadows. The flashlights gave a

Shadow Puppets in the Maya Mountains in Belize

softer, more directed light, and could be more diffused or defined depending on whether the flashlight holder moved closer to or farther from the screen. The puppet master and the flashlight holder had to work in concert, moving together in a duet of light and voice.

On the final night of our week in Belize, the teachers invited their families and friends from the community to come to the play. It was a huge success, and the teachers told us they would use this strategy in their classrooms so their kids could become catalysts for community action.

Shadows, Social Studies, and the Constitution

Shadow puppets are also an effective strategy to help kids understand historical social issues. After studying the Revolutionary War period and the creation of the Constitution, my students use the shadow-puppet strategy to demonstrate their understanding of the Bill of Rights. In groups of three, they develop short plays that identify the problem or issue addressed by one of the amendments. They create characters who demonstrate what might have happened if we had lost this right in the past or what might happen if we lost the right today.

Or another example. My kids read a biography of Harriet Tubman. They also learn about other experiences with slavery from sources as diverse as Harriet Beecher Stowe's *Uncle Tom's Cabin* and Julius Lester's *To Be a Slave*. After reading picture books, first-person accounts, and chapter books and watching videotapes and filmstrips, my kids create shadow-puppet plays retelling the stories they have learned. We devote a week to this, as we do with "The Three Precious Pearls," but this time the kids write their own scripts and each group does a different play. I encourage the kids to connect their plays to the Civil Rights amendments (the Thirteenth, Fourteenth, Fifteenth, and Twenty-fourth), which I paraphrase for them. An example scenario based on and a paraphrase of the Thirteenth Amendment is provided in Appendix 6-2.

Kamishibai: Japanese Story Cards

Kamishibai (kah-mee-shee-bye), a unique form of Japanese storytelling, is another authentic cultural strategy. (I am indebted to my good friend Marte Peet, of Lockwood Elementary, for sharing it with me.) I like this strategy for the art involved as much as for the reading and language arts connections.

The kamishibai man was a candy seller and storyteller who announced his presence in a village by clapping two wooden blocks together. Children, hearing the sound, would come running to hear his stories. But first, he would sell candy. Those children who bought candy got to sit in the front rows; those who did not had to find places farther back.

The kamishibai man illustrated his stories with story cards, on the back of which was written the script of the story. Traditionally, he placed the cards on a small stage, often located on the back of the bicycle he rode from village to village. He would stand beside the stage, telling the story. Sometimes he even acted it out. Early on, the story cards were hand drawn and very beautiful to look at.

Often the stories were in serial form, and children eagerly awaited

Kindergarten Buddies Listen to Caitlyn's Kamishibai

the next installment, just as children in this country in the forties did with the old Saturday-matinee serials. After television was introduced in Japan in 1953, the kamishibai man faded away.

There has recently been renewed interest in kamishibai story cards in Japan. Japanese teachers and librarians are using them in their classrooms as an alternative to reading stories. I use story cards in my classroom to check reading comprehension, provide oral communication practice, and develop visual/spatial intelligence while adding to the students' artistic skills.

Here's how the strategy works, step by step:

1. Read (or write) a story.
2. Identify the four, five, or six most important parts of the story.
3. Draw illustrations of just those important parts. Use full-page pictures, at least a foot square, and color in the background. Be sure to use large figures, so the cards will be able to be used with large groups.

4. Write a rough draft of the story. Use dialogue, like a play, as much as possible. Be sure to tell the whole story. Share your rough draft with a buddy and get suggestions for improvement.

5. Word-process the draft and proofread it out loud. Make corrections and print out a final copy.

6. Cut the story into sections to match your pictures. Glue the writing onto the back of your pictures. (Traditionally, the script for picture 1 is glued to the back of the last story card, the script for picture 2 is affixed to the back of story card 1, the script for picture 3 to the back of story card 2, and so on.)

7. Put the cards in order. Place the pack of cards upright on a table or in your lap.

8. Show card 1 to the audience. Read the text that accompanies the picture from the back of the last card. When finished with the story for card 1, pull card 1 aside and place it at the back of the pack, revealing card 2. Read the story for that card as written on the back of card 1, and so on through the story.

9. Perform as a kamishibai man or woman for at least three different audiences—peers, adults, younger kids—and write a reflective piece about the differences you noticed among the three groups.

Teachers can obtain kamishibai sets from Kamishibai for Kids, P.O. Box 20069, Park West Station, New York, NY 10025-1510, telephone and fax 212-662-5836. The text is written in both Japanese and English. Having a model certainly helps the children understand what they are being asked to create. I have a set for a New Year's story, "*Hats for the Jizo*," and read it to my students the first day back from winter break. I use the story as a way to compare Oshogatsu, the Japanese New Year, to how my students celebrate the holiday. Then I ask them to use the story cards to share something they read over the winter break (all my students are expected to read at least one chapter book). This strategy lets me know what the kids are reading, and often piques class interest in a particular book, a certain author, or a new genre.

Yakima Native American Time Ball

Time is a relationship between events,
Kept fresh in the memory by selected objects on knotted hemp.
Connection is as vital as Separation.
The strand is begun by a woman at her marriage.
By the time she is a grandmother,
The unity of life is wrapped
    and remembered
    in a Time Ball.
        (From *The Yakima Time Ball*, a brochure compiled
        by Yakima Nation Media Program, 1984,
        P.O. Box 151, Toppenish, WA 98948)

Like all Native American nations, the Yakima, who reside on the east side of what is now Washington State, have a long history, much of it oral. But they did have a unique way of recording bits of the past. New brides used string made out of hemp weed to record their life history, starting with their courtship. They tied a bead or a knot into the string to represent each important event in their lives. The resulting ball of string, or *ititamat*, which means "counting the days" or "counting calendar," was small during the first year but grew in size as the women got older. Sometimes the string was divided into twenty-five-year lengths to make it easier to handle. When the women were very old, they could pick up one of their lifetime balls of string and, by the knots and beads, recall not only what had happened in the past but when it happened. They could recount when their children were born, when they moved, or when they became grandmothers. When the women died, their time ball was buried with them.

Being able to create and read time lines is a social studies skill. Organizing events in sequence demonstrates logical-mathematical intelligence. Classifying events is a science skill. When I read the two-page brochure about the Yakima time ball I thought, Here's a highly kinesthetic and concrete way to help my students work with time lines while honoring a Native American custom through thoughtful replication.

144

Deciding Where to Place Each Symbol

"A Relationship Between Events"

In the fall, as we studied Jamestown and the early colonization of the East Coast by Europeans, I had the children tell me what they knew about Pocahontas. Of course, most of them had seen the Disney movie and regaled me with this highly romantic version of her life. I introduced them to other versions, including Jean Fritz's *The Double*

Life of Pocahantas and an October 1995 *Storyworks* article that offered different points of view.

As a class, we constructed a time line of Pocahontas's life. Then each child began a personal time line. The hardest part for most of the kids was keeping "the relationship between events" fairly accurate. Marking off equidistant segments and labeling them by year helped them stay on track. Some of the children took their time lines home to find out about important events in their lives or to get more accurate dates.

Keeping Memories Fresh

Immediately after winter break, I like my students to think about their past and connect it to their future by setting goals. This year I decided we'd replicate Yakima time balls as a concrete way to represent their reflection and their dreams. During parent conferences in the late fall, I ask the parents of each of my students to identify one or more expectations they have for their child during the year. Their responses range from "be a better speller" and "improve her handwriting" to "read more without me making him" to "love to learn." The first week back after the break, I meet individually with each student. We identify what it is his or her parents expect and then make a plan for how the student might begin meeting this expectation. When conferences are over, I announce to the kids that we are going to do some goal setting the following week and they need to be thinking of at least two goals they have for themselves. At least one has to be something that is related to being a student and that can be accomplished between January and June.

Beginning at the Beginning

We begin creating the time balls by referring to the personal time lines they made in the fall. Each child has identified from eight to ten significant events. I ask the kids to look at their events and see if they can classify them into categories. Birthdays, pets, moves, and siblings figure in many of my students' lives. We decide that knots will stand for years. Using a new kind of clay that air dries, the students fashion

Stringing a Time Ball

beads for each of the events in their lives, shaping the bead according to the category of the event.

Since my students are fourth and fifth graders, I give them each twelve feet of string, each foot representing a year. When they finish putting their beads and knots at the appropriate points on the string, I ask them to think about their goals. In addition to the two they have identified already, I ask them to add one long-range goal, something they'd like to accomplish by the time they are twelve.

Each student then creates three more beads representing their goals and attaches them on the end of their string.

Sitting in small groups, the students remember their history for their peers as they unwrap their time ball. Each bead inspires a story, each knot elicits a response from the listeners. A warmth is generated and the unity of life is shared.

Endnote

Our first grandchild was born a year ago. Unfortunately, she lives in Seoul, Korea, with our daughter Tia, and son-in-law Scott. We don't get to see her very often. I'm starting a time ball for her so I'll have a tangible reminder of things I want to tell her when she is older. I feel more connected to her now that I have started the time ball. Parents of my students tell me the time ball has become an important part of

Important Life Events All Wrapped Up!

their family history as well, encouraging the family to recollect together where they have been and plan together where they are going, both literally and figuratively. I also think the time balls might be the perfect impetus for some powerful poetry or songs. We'll try that later in the year.

Appendix 6-1: The Chinese Screen

- Create a threefold screen. Label one section PLUS, one section MINUS, and one section INTERESTING.
- Think about all you did to prepare and present *The Three Precious Pearls*. Using both words and pictures, list the *pluses*, or positive things about this activity; the *minuses*, or things you didn't enjoy; and some *interesting* aspects of the experience.
- You must have at least eight separate items.

The grading criteria are:

thoughtful responses (50 percent)

presentation (40 percent)

completed on time (10 percent).

Note: This is my interpretation and implementation of deBono's (1992) PMI model as one way of assessing creativity.

Appendix 6-2: Thirteenth Amendment Scenario

Setting: The living room in Mrs. Sammon's plantation home.

Mrs. Sammon: Trudy! Trudy! Come here.

Trudy: Yes, Missus Sammon.

Mrs. Sammon: Trudy, did you hear that Elvinia's young son, Ethan, was sold downriver?

Trudy: Yes, mam, I did.

Mrs. Sammon: Trudy, how long have you been with us?

Trudy: Oh, all my life, Missus, and all my mammy's life, too.

Mrs. Sammon: Well, Trudy, Master Sammon is very upset. He saw your son, Timothy, meeting with some other young men behind the barn.

Trudy: Timothy, mam?

Mrs. Sammon: Yes, Timothy. Now, I want to remember how many years you have been with us. I wouldn't want that to change. Make sure Timothy understands that my husband doesn't want change either.

Trudy: Yes, Missus Sammon. *(Trudy exits singing)* "Steal away, steal away, steal away home to Jesus."

Paraphrase: No persons of the United States shall be placed into slavery or bondage against their will unless they are being punished for a crime they were found guilty of doing in the United States. (Adapted from the *Elementary Law-Related Education Resource Guide*, Cleveland City School District.)

Bibliography for Multicultural Literature

BARRY, DAVID, adaptor. 1994. *The Rajah's Rice: A Mathematical Folktale from India.* New York: W. H. Freeman. With vivid illustrations, this picture book presents the same mathematical axiom presented in *The Grain of Rice*, by Helana Pittman, but sets it in a different culture. Offers great opportunities for comparison and contrast.

BAYLOR, BYRD. 1965/1992. *One Small Blue Bead.* New York: Charles Scribner's Sons. A beautifully rhymed story about the power of knowledge and the strength of the group. A great book to share with kids in transition, especially classes moving from elementary to middle school or junior high.

BRUCHAC, JOSEPH, and JONATHAN LONDON. 1992. *Thirteen Moons on Turtle's Back.* New York: Philomel. Poems based on Cherokee, Cree, and Sioux legends celebrating the seasons of the year. Students also enjoy the striking illustrations by Thomas Locker.

DEMI. 1996. *A Grain of Rice.* New York: Scholastic. Set in fifteenth-century China, this story not only engages readers of all ages, but teaches them a little about mathematics as well, through the powers of two.

DORRIS, MICHAEL. 1996. *Sees Behind Trees.* New York: Hyperion. "Before Pocahontas, there was a boy named Sees Behind Trees," begins Dorris's rebuttal to the romanticization of sixteenth-century America. It is the story of one boy who turns a handicap into an advantage during his coming of age in a Powhatan village.

FRITZ, JEAN. 1983. *The Double Life of Pocahantas.* New York: Puffin. A biography of a famous Native American woman and the roles she played in two very different cultures.

GRUTMAN, JEWEL H., and GAY MATTHAEI. 1994. *The Ledgerbook of Thomas Blue Eagle.* Charlottesville, VA: Thomasson-Grant. A fictional account of a young Sioux warrior who is placed in the Carlisle Indian School, this book is inspired by remarkable pictographs of the Plains Indians that were created in the late nineteenth century.

JONES, HETTIE, editor. 1971. *The Trees Stand Shining.* New York: Dial. Thirty-two brief songs, chants, and lullabies are translated from diverse native nations and provide powerful examples of their respect for and harmony with nature. Beautifully illustrated by Robert Andrew Parker.

PATERSON, KATHERINE. 1975. *The Master Puppeteer.* New York: HarperTrophy. A perfect chapter book to intrigue middle school readers while providing some insight into *bunraku,* a form of Japanese puppet theater.

SAY, ALLEN. 1993. *Grandfather Say.* Boston: Houghton Mifflin. One of my favorite books to use while studying immigration. It is also a story that needs to be told about one man who came to this country from Japan but didn't stay.

TOMPERT, ANN. 1990. *Grandfather Tang's Story: A Tale Told with Tangrams.* New York: Crown. Tangrams are ancient Chinese puzzles used in storytelling. Logical-mathematical intelligence is challenged as the storyteller uses the same seven shapes, called *tans,* to create a multitude of pictures. Each piece must touch another but none can overlap.

VELARDE, PABLITA. 1989. *Old Father Story Teller.* Santa Fe: Clear Light. An outstanding American Indian artist, Velarde has selected six memorable tribal tales to retell and illustrate from her Santa Clara Pueblo heritage.

WALLIS, VELMA. 1993. *Two Old Women*. New York: HarperCollins. An attention-keeping read-aloud Alaskan legend of betrayal, courage, and survival. Not to be missed by either adult or child.

————. 1996. *Bird Girl and the Man who Followed the Sun*. Fairbanks: Epicenter. An Athabaskan Indian legend from Alaska, this is an ideal read-aloud for older students who can debate the choices the author made while writing this story and extrapolate the values hidden within.

WOODS, NANCY. 1993. *Spirit Walker*. New York: Delacorte. Poems celebrating the courage, determination, and faith of Native Americans that appeal to middle school and junior high readers. Paintings by Frank Howell are especially magnificent.

YEP, LAURENCE. 1989. *The Rainbow People* and *Tongues of Jade*. New York: HarperTrophy. Both of these books are collections of Chinese folktales that were passed on orally for generations. These were collected primarily from immigrants who recently settled in the United States. Intermediate-grade kids love these stories, either having them read aloud or reading them alone.

YOLEN, JANE. 1988. *The Emperor and the Kite*. New York: Philomel. This charming picture book inspires exploration of the history of Chinese kite making.

SEVEN

Constitutional Visions: Connecting the Constitution, Kids, Science, Civics, and Social Studies

Social studies programs should include experiences that provide for the study of: how people create and change structures of power, authority, and governance; interactions among individuals, groups, and institutions; relationships among science, technology, and society; and the ideals, principles, and practices of citizenship in a democratic republic.

—NCSS Standard

I had been teaching fifth-grade social studies for a few years, and several parts of the social studies curriculum were coming together quite nicely. I had a clear picture of what it was I was supposed to teach. I knew what to emphasize and what to ignore. My resources were multiplying. My classroom bookshelves held a wide range of literature—chapter books and picture books, fiction and nonfiction—that more often than not touched on what I was supposed to teach, early U.S. history. My audiotape library was filled with stories from a myriad of American cultures and events in our history as well as songs providing insight into issues of the day. My videotape collection was eclectic, dealing with major historical moments and capturing people, places, and events. My kids were integrating writing, reading, thinking, and drawing as they constructed their own understanding of the past. They were practicing day-to-day citizenship as they worked in groups, developed problem-solving strategies, and dealt with the little annoyances group projects sometimes give rise to. Yet something wasn't right.

The problem was the Constitution and the Bill of Rights. These documents are two of the most important in our history. Yet when I introduced them to elementary students à la carte, they caused glazed-eye disease and head-on-the-desk syndrome. How could I help my students not only understand these documents of democracy but care about them and the principles they stand for?

The lessons I was conducting, usually following the textbook, were awful. If my goal was deliberately to kill any student interest in the Constitution, I was succeeding. I seldom used the text for any other unit we studied—I considered it a resource book, a handy reference, a quick way to preview a topic. All my other units were broadly structured, allowed for personalization, and integrated knowing, doing, and feeling. But I was tied to the text when I taught the Constitution.

That was the problem. Instead of a connected, integrated unit, I was teaching a lesson or two—isolated, independent, and incredibly unidimensional. Focusing on the specific content of the documents, I ignored two critical ingredients for learner engagement: context and involvement. Two-hundred-year-old problems might have been mildly interesting to some of the kids but certainly did not ignite the imagination and the energy of the whole class.

My solution was to retain the documents but to change the time to the future and change the place to space: we would take the U.S. Constitution into space.

Starting with Assumptions

To begin the unit, I ask pairs of children to take one of the space colony assumptions in Appendix 7-1 and report on it to the class. They present the information in their own words, and we discuss the topic under their leadership. Every child in the classroom has a copy of the space assumptions, and after each presentation, the important information is highlighted.

When the space assumptions have been discussed, the kids close their eyes and join me on a guided fantasy of traveling into space (some possible prompts are included in Appendix 7-2). Asking the kids to imagine some of the assumptions we have just discussed builds their interest in what they'll be doing next.

After the guided fantasy, the kids draw a picture of their idea of a community in space. I play "spacey" music softly in the background while the children draw their images of life in space. I've put out all the books I have been able to check out of the library on space and the solar system. Every windowsill, chalkboard tray, and tabletop is covered with picture books and chapter books, reference books and science fiction. I've hung charts of our solar system, pictures of space flights from NASA, and diagrams of our constellation. As children finish their drawings, they gravitate toward the books, some browsing, others burrowing. What a wonderful first day in space!

Getting the Group Together

When the kids enter the room the next morning, they discover their desks have been moved. Since we frequently move our desks to facilitate the activity of the moment, it's no big deal. This time they are grouped into pods of six desks each, the largest groups they've encountered all year. This is deliberate: I want establishing the space colonies to stretch their social participation. These kids have established patterns for working quite well with three and four people and are now ready to try a larger group.

We begin with oral reading. Jill Paton Walsh's *The Green Book* is a brief and gripping story about the last spaceship to leave an ailing Earth. Her writing style is stunning, terse, and clear. The story immediately engages the kids' attention: Walsh poses problems the colonists meet and pushes the imagination into another dimension. My kids are now ready to go into space. "Working in your groups, create space colonies. We'll begin that process by sharing the drawings from yesterday."

The General Data Disc

Using an overhead transparency, we review the general data disc (see the photo on page 157), a useful strategy that helps focus the kids' energy and gives their groups a concrete goal. Some of the kids notice that the information asked for is similar to that on the general data sheet they used when they did their state report. The students are applying previous practice to a new setting. (See Appendix 7-3 for focus questions to help them get started.)

Before they begin, we discuss procedure and how they will make decisions if there are disagreements (and there will be). It's up to each group to work out their own plan, but we list the possibilities:

- The most who want it (majority rule).
- Everyone agrees (consensus).
- Each person gets a turn (pool and pick)—see Appendix 7-4.
- Strongest gets his way (dictatorship).
- Get mad and quit (not acceptable).

Amazingly, most of the groups get going and function pretty well, but usually there is one that has tough slugging. For that group, the pool-and-pick strategy seems to help.

As we finish this stage of our journey into space, we decide the colonists might want to think of a name for their new colony by the next meeting. Then I designate a large section of the bulletin board for each group to use as a "repository," and the kids begin to display their discs and other colony-related material.

The afternoon is filled with creativity. Some students design the vehicle they will use to travel from Earth to their new colony. These drawings show both the outside of the craft and the interior layout of the ship. Other students extend their mapping skills by drawing a map of their space colony and using a legend to indicate physical features, natural resources, chief products, and population density. Still other kids develop a coded language using only geometric shapes or numbers. One student writes a weather report for his colony. Kids ask me whether they can do things at home for their colony and bring them to school. I say, "Don't ask me. Ask your group."

The Cultural Data Disc

The divergent paths each group takes regarding general data are fascinating, and I'm impressed by the serious demeanor of the presenters and the delight of the listeners as they share their combined visions of living in space. To promote generalizations, I introduce the cultural data disc, which is designed to emphasize the relationships between environment and culture. The cultural disc is affixed to the blank core of the larger general data disc by a brad placed at the center, which allows the inner disc to rotate.

I ask the groups to rotate the general data disc, paying particular attention to the natural resources section. "How could natural resources influence the shelter you build on your colony? the clothing you wear? the traditions, like holidays and favorite sports, you observe? Would natural resources influence the kind of food you eat?

Creating a Double Data Disc Is Fun

Would it affect the economy of your colony and the education your kind must have to be productive?"

Next we move to climate, speculating about how it would influence cultural activities, from housing to jobs. I elicit examples from my students, such as that South Pacific cultures use palm leaves for shelter and for clothing while Inuits use hide and fur. In this way, each group proceeds around the disc, making generalizations about the specific relationships between their space environment and spacekind culture. (A nearly completed double data disc is shown in Figure 7-1)

I tell my students, "Shelter is one of earthkind's primary needs. We can assume it will also be very important to spacekind as well. Keeping in mind your colony's climate, natural resources, size, physical features, population density, and chief products, design an appropriate shelter to live in. Designs should be in color, carefully drawn, and labeled where necessary. Completed drawings should be displayed in the repository."

Spacekind Paper Dolls

With the environment and the culture firmly and cooperatively envisioned, we explore the kind of jobs people will have in space. The recent PBS program *Living and Working in Space: The Countdown Has Begun* is an excellent resource. To personalize this adventure, each student creates a paper doll of himself or herself working in space. First they create the dolls. I provide a pattern for kids to work from if they choose. Some teachers have their kids trace each other, life size. Some years my kids "dress" one of their peers in their spacekind native regalia.

To focus thinking on working in space, the kids create job descriptions for their spacekind persona. First they analyze several job description formats. They notice the language used, the brief, straightforward style, and the information usually given: title, location, qualifications, specific responsibilities, and salary. Then they write the job description.

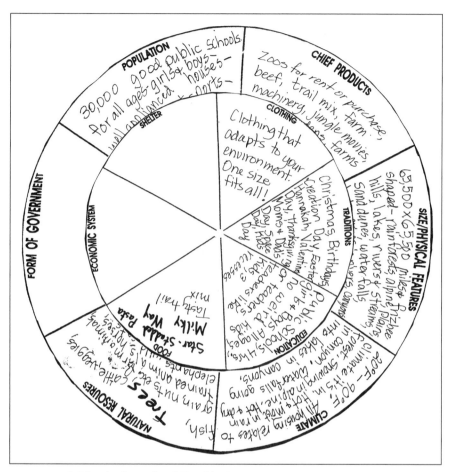

FIG. 7-1:   *A Nearly Completed Double Data Disc*

Space Journal

Using *The Green Book* as a model, the kids begin writing their own space journal using the computers in our computer lab. We decide on at least five entries: leaving Earth, the trip, the landing, exploration, and settling in. Weekly work on the journals includes writing and adding graphics depicting the trip. Caitlyn's journal entry on the following page is an example.

Earthkind and Spacekind Go for a Walk

January 6, 2006
Dear Diary,

Today at 1:12, I turned eleven. I got this marbled notebook for my birthday. My dad didn't plan for me to use this as a diary but that's how it turned out. You already know I am eleven so let me tell you more about myself. My name is Alexandra Kathryn Arrow but everyone calls me Alex. My eyes are green in some lights and gray in others. I like to wear my long brown hair in a French braid.

I have a nine, soon-to-be ten, year old brother, Bob, who is taller than me. I think he's a brat. I also have a sixteen year old sister, Carmen. She is very pretty. My mother died when Bob was born.

I got some bad news this morning. The government has chosen six families to leave earth and go into space. We were one of the six. Dad didn't think it all that bad, but I do. He explained to me that for quite awhile scientists have been thinking of ways to live in space and they have finally figured out something. They picked out six families to try it out. In my mind, I saw a scientist grabbing six hamsters to try an experiment! People, these days!

But what really got me was Dad's last sentence, "We're leaving tomorrow." Outrageous!

"We are going on the best ship they can find," my father said. I am comforted by that thought.

Everybody's Got to Eat

Celestial Snack Cooking Contest

- Every space colony needs at least one favorite snack food.
- Consider your resources and environment.
- Think about your lifestyle.
- Create a perfect snack for your colony.
- Give your snack an appropriate name.
- Bring a large enough sample so we can all have a taste.
- Bring in the recipe.
- Be sure to clean the kitchen when you're done!
- You may work alone or work in a group.
- Contest is open to all citizens of any space colony.

The more snacks, the more we eat! —Old celestial saying

What a homework assignment! Working in groups or individually, each student creates a favorite food for the Celestial Snack Cooking Contest. (This assignment is most successful when parents are given plenty of notice.)

To prepare for the assignment, we review the general data discs, noting climate, physical features, and natural resources, and talk about how food might reflect some of those conditions. The kids consider attributes of a celestial snack: lightweight, travels well, easily packaged, plentiful raw materials, easily manufactured, and popular. I always try to sneak in "nutritious," but the kids usually catch me and rule it out!

Looking at a sample recipe, we set the standards for what must be included in their recipes: ingredients, amounts used, procedure, cooking temperature, resulting quantity. I also stress that they need to make the snack with adult supervision and must clean the kitchen when they are finished. Students who for one reason or another cannot bring in a sample may just bring in a recipe. Teachers who don't want to deal with food in the classroom have successfully turned this activity into a creative writing assignment by having the class create a cookbook for chefs in space.

On the day of the snack judging, we start by figuring how many snacks we have to taste. Each student gets a construction-paper place mat, which he or she divides into as many squares as there are snacks, numbering each square sequentially. The first snack is introduced. Using a word processor, I type the number 1 and the entry's name, and the kids can see it on the monitor. The contestant then passes the snack out to all the other kids and they place it in the number 1 square on their place mat. Then the second child introduces her snack, I record its name after the number 2, and she passes out samples. And so it goes until all the snacks are passed out.

Now comes the good part. The kids try bites and sips and nibbles of each snack, sharing observations with their group members. While the kids are enjoying the snacks, I hurry down to the copy machine and make copies of the list of entries for all the kids. After about fifteen minutes they are ready to vote.

Everybody Wins

To make this activity more of a celebration of creativity than a competition, we use a system called the "Delphi technique" to determine the most popular snack. Here's how it works. Each student judges the snacks individually, giving the favorite snack 25 points. The second-best snack receives 20 points, third-best, 15 points, fourth-best, 10 points, and fifth-best, 5 points. All the rest of the snacks get one point.

When the individual judging is completed, each group tallies their points. The groups report their point totals to me and I write them on the board by the appropriate snack. The class then tallies the total points for each snack. The snack with the most points wins the Celestial Snack Award, but every snack garners points and everybody feels like a winner.

Hands-on Science Investigation

For a few days, the kids explore living in space through hands-on science investigations.

First, they simulate weightlessness by filling a plastic tub with water and trying to screw different-sized nuts and bolts together under water using only one hand. Ben has this to say afterward: "This experiment is much harder than it looks. It required lots of patience and coordination. I think it would have been easier if we had done it in air instead of water, because the water simulates a little bit of weightlessness. This makes it harder to get everything where you want it to be. Another observation is that big bolts were easier than smaller ones. I also noticed that all of my times improved, which shows once you do it for awhile, it gets easier."

The kids also simulate docking in space by making a hoop out of a coat hanger and hanging it from the ceiling with a string. Then, after swinging the hoop in an orbit, they try to toss objects of various weights through the moving hoop. Bean bags, tennis balls, cotton balls present different challenges. Andrew comments, "One time when I tried it, I hit the edge of the hoop and it started to spin fast. I can't imagine what would happen if that happened in space. There are so many things that could change the way a docking occurs. One variable is speed. If you are going very fast, it would be quite hard to dock well. It also takes practice. The more you practice the better the dock will be."

The kids also research planets or moons of their choice, calculate their weight on each planet, and carry out a space experiment with seeds to see which way their roots would grow in weightless space. Kara noted, "The gravity roots grew straight. The space seed roots grew all curly."

Jigsaw Toward Unity

Historians identify several issues facing the Confederation after the Revolutionary War: no taxing power, therefore no money; inflation; tariff wars; jealousy and quarreling among the states; different trade regulations in each state; conflicts over debts, such as Shay's Rebellion; and disrespect from nations like Spain and England, who were sure that self-government would never work.

Our discussion now revolves around these problems. The kids have some good ideas about why these issues surfaced. We speculate about whether these or similar problems could happen in our space colonies. Reactions range from disbelief to excited whispers about the construction of possible weapons to "blow the others away." The atmosphere suddenly changes. Some children are charged up. Others are intimidated. We explore these feelings and discuss what to do.

"What do you think our forefathers did in their time of crisis? Here they had won the war but were falling apart before becoming a country." Answers gradually focus in: "Had a meeting." "Got together and talked." "Made some agreements." "Decided on government." After much discussion, the kids decide they want to come together, form a space nation, and work together. In an effort to blend the colonies into a single entity, representatives from various space colonies will meet and design one of the following for our nation in space: a flag, a map, an anthem, a curriculum, money, a holiday, a mascot, and a sport.

I jigsaw the group formations, and the kids busily get to work in their new groups, sharing ideas and coming to agreements. (To jigsaw, number the kids in each group starting with a number 1. Then place all the 1's in a new group, the 2's, the 3's, and so on.) The results are shared. For the rest of the unit, we open our day singing our new space anthem.

Biosphere III

Our room is transformed. No longer an ordinary classroom, it has become a place in space. The catalyst? A large bubble made of plastic and duct tape, kept inflated by a fourteen-inch fan (see Appendix 7-5 for directions). It doesn't sound very exciting, but it is. Large enough for forty students to sit inside, the biosphere is the meeting place for our constitutional convention.

We begin by identifying the characteristics of good governments and bad governments. Meeting in colonial groups, the kids list characteristics of a bad government: "Bad governments don't care about the people." "Bad governments punish people unfairly." "Bad governments tell people where they have to live." The lists are shared, and as each characteristic is verbalized, we explore: What exactly makes this action bad? Is it unfair? Does it treat people in the same situation

This Is the Beginning of a New Country in Space!

differently? Does it deprive people of freedom, their property, or other rights they consider important?

The discussion moves on to, How would a good government handle this situation? How would you define a good government?

Good Governments and Bad Governments

More than two thousand years ago, Greek philosophers such as Plato and Aristotle classified governments in a way that is still useful. In trying to identify the best kind or kinds of government, they arrived at the following definitions:

> Good governments have rulers who care about the community. They rule according to law. For example, if the law says pickpockets must spend from six months to one year in jail, then all persons found guilty of picking pockets will serve that time in jail, no matter who they are.
>
> Bad governments have rulers who care about special groups and not about the whole community. They do not follow the law; instead they do whatever they please. For example, even if the law says that all pickpockets must spend from six months to one year in jail, the rulers may say their pickpocketing friends don't have to spend any time in jail and that other pickpockets may have to spend five years in jail because they didn't pay a bribe to the government.
>
> Whether a government is ruled by one person, by a few people, or by many is not important. Even a government ruled by a king or queen can be a good government if it is ruled for the good of the community and according to law.

Three Branches of Government

It's time for a microlesson on our own government. Since we held a mock presidential election in the fall, my students have a pretty good understanding of the executive branch but are, for the most part, confused about the legislative branch and clueless about the judicial branch. They need some information before analyzing the United States Constitution.

A focus sheet assists our discussion of each branch, matching the major players and their responsibilities as well as identifying a few checks and balances between the branches.

The Preamble

Meeting in the biosphere, we begin by comparing the original preamble to a simplified one:

> We the people of the United States, in order to have a better government, to treat everyone fairly, to have a peaceful country, to defend the country from enemies, to live in a comfortable way, and to make sure people are free now and forever, make this Constitution for the United States of America.

The kids match phrases, such as "insure domestic Tranquillity" to "have a peaceful country," and we discuss the language and its meaning and speculate about why our forefathers thought each attribute important enough to mention.

Then I read selections from books about the Constitutional Convention aloud to the kids, and they hypothesize what it must have been like. Our biosphere helps us create a feeling similar to that in Philadelphia, when the participants met behind closed doors and shuttered windows, an intense and dynamic environment.

The Constitution

The groups jigsaw once again, new members in each group, to discuss a simplified constitution (see Appendix 7-6) and rewrite it for life in space. Once again, each student represents his or her colony. Five groups work well, since I divide the Constitution into five sections: (1) Preamble, (2) Article I—The Legislative Branch, (3) Article II—The Executive Branch, (4) Article III—The Judicial Branch, and (5) Articles IV–VII—The States, Amendments, the Highest Law, and Ratification. "Read your assigned article and decide as a group, Can we take this Constitution into space or does it need to be rewritten? If it does, rewrite it to fit our new space nation." The questions in

Finishing Up Space Journal Entries Before Entering the Biosphere

Appendix 7-7 will help the students conduct their discussion and make their decisions.

The Constitutional Process

The process of analyzing and rewriting the articles of the Constitution to fit the space colonies is one that needs time, lots of talk, and sometimes, mediation. Some groups get right to work and seemingly breeze through the task, sharing thoughtful statements and listening carefully, compromising and collaborating in the best way possible. Other groups can't seem to get started. They need a gentle but firm nudge. The focus questions seem to be most helpful to them. Still other groups simulate the outbreak of World War III. Argumentative, combative, and each determined to have it his or her way, these are the kids who need help in the art of compromise, guidance in the gift of consensus. While these children frequently are quite adept at expressing their personal convictions, they have difficulty adjusting their own behavior to fit the dynamics of the group and seldom seem to recognize the mutual relationship between human beings in satisfying one another's needs.

Deciding how disagreements will be settled is critical. I often use a modification of the pool-and-pick technique with groups who have great difficulty compromising. Sometimes, just getting the group started and sitting near them while they deliberate helps. A hand on a shoulder, a raised eyebrow, or a gentle shake of the head can frequently decelerate impulsive and inconsiderate behavior and facilitate an agreement of sorts.

Each year my students discover what hard work it is, this struggle to get more than one person's ideas discussed, shaped, fine-tuned, agreed on, and written in such a way that the message is clear and precise. Each year my students develop an appreciation for the men who met to draft the document we still use. They imagine the arguments that must have occurred, the agreements that must have been struck, the frustration with which the Framers must have walked home each evening. My kids report that they think about our space nation constitution at night and plan how they might get other kids to accept their ideas.

The constitutional process needs more than one or two separate days. Short periods of time, about a half hour each, work in my classroom, and spreading the task over several days seems to encourage thoughtful analysis and stimulate creativity while fostering understanding.

When each group has completed its task, they enter their Article on the computer. Soon, I am able to announce that the first draft of their document has just been returned from the printer and it is necessary for the authors to share their ideas and evaluate the document as a whole. They begin by reading silently, marking points they want to discuss or question.

As they read, I write the words *consensus* and *compromise* on the board, along with their definitions: a collective opinion or general agreement about some matter, and the process of coming to an agreement or settlement by means of making concessions. The children determine which definition matches which word, and we discuss the difference. I remind the kids that when the authors of our Constitution were writing it, they spent the entire summer of 1787 in Philadelphia, drafting, redrafting, and trying to come to consensus on the best Constitution by way of debate and compromise. The fifty-five delegates represented different states in the Union, just as the students represent different colonies in our space nation.

Next, we read the document together, aloud, and articulate those issues that still need to be resolved. I am always amazed by the high level of discourse and am usually pleased by the civility that permeates the discussions. Creative and critical thinking is very much in evidence as the students verbalize their ideals and explore concepts related to the U.S. Constitution and their imaginary space colonies. We list the benefits and costs of living in space and compare them to life on Earth.

As agreements are reached and consensus is established, we make changes directly to the document. A word processing program connected to a monitor that everyone in the class can see makes the computer not only efficient but a powerful teaching device as well. My students appreciate the space age's answer to the quill pen even more as the class becomes a "Committee on Style," correcting any grammatical, spelling, or other errors they have noticed. Once again, words matter. So do stylistic conventions.

When the final changes have been made, the students have an opportunity to sign the document as an indication of their approval and most of them do, just as most of the framers of the U.S. Constitution did. We send home copies with their signatures and share their document with the principal, the local Board of School Directors, and our PTSA board. Appendix 7-8 is a copy of the space colony constitution my students created.

Adding the Bill of Rights

Once the constitution has been written, we look at the concept of "rights." "How would you define 'rights'? Is freedom a right? Is having enough food to eat a right? What does the word mean to you?" Rights can be classified into many categories, but for our purposes, rights mean generally accepted principles of fairness and justice.

To help students see the need for the Bill of Rights, I pose a number of hypothetical situations:

1. Tofu steals a piece of candy from the corner store. He is arrested and taken to jail, where the police sergeant decides that the punishment will be to cut off Tofu's right index finger. Are Tofu's rights being abused? (This would be cruel and unusual punishment, which is not allowed under the Eighth Amendment.)

2. The government of the space colony has manufactured an army of robots, called "terminators," to enforce the laws. These robots are programmed to seize any citizen suspected of committing a crime and take him or her to jail. Arwen is shopping at the Astro-Mart when she is suddenly scooped up by a terminator and whisked away to jail. She has no idea what she is accused of and what she can do to be released. Have Arwen's rights been ignored? (This raises questions about unreasonable search and seizure, prohibited by our Fourth Amendment, and fair trial procedures, protected by the Fifth and Sixth amendments. Should robots be able to arrest anyone suspected of a crime? Can robots make reasoned judgments about probable cause, as police officers are required to do?)

3. Gandolf is a student at Cosmos Middle School. He has started a school newspaper that covers school sports events, the latest in computer games, and news about the local community. His first issue includes an article about the upcoming visit of earthkind to evaluate the school. The article is critical of some of the school policies, such as requiring all students to learn earthspeak. Before the first issue even comes out, the principal tells him that school newspapers are not allowed and all copies of the newspaper will be burned. What are Gandolf's rights in this situation? (This raises the issue of free speech and free press. There is a whole line of cases about school newspapers, and when they may be controlled

or censored by school authorities. In the case above, the principal is not allowing any type of newspaper and censorship seems based on the criticism of school policy. In *Hazelwood v. Kuhlmeier*, decided by the U.S. Supreme Court in 1988, the Court held that the school administration has editorial control over a school newspaper when it is part of a regular class. Educators must show their actions in censoring or controlling the content of the paper were reasonably related to legitimate educational concerns.)

4. Angela is a member of the Interplanetary Church of Pluto. The space colony outlaws her church, and tells Angela she must join the Intergalactic Church of Venus. Are Angela's rights being protected? (This would be a violation of the First Amendment of the U.S. Bill of Rights, which protects the free exercise of religion.)

After discussing these hypothetical situations, the class brainstorms other rights they want protected by their new constitution. After we have created a long list, the kids regroup themselves into their original space colonies, reviewing their original data discs to see if any other rights might need protection. Each space colony cooperatively prepares a list of rights they feel must be protected. When the initial energy and excitement begin to dwindle and ideas are on the wane, I hand out a simplified Bill of Rights (see Appendix 7-9).

After completing their list, each group cooperatively ranks each right in order of importance to them. We develop the Galactic Bill of Rights by asking one group to read their first priority aloud while someone types it into the computer, displaying it on the classroom monitor. Then the second group reads their first priority, and so on. If a group's first priority has already been read, they read their second priority. This process of round-robin reading and sharing continues until a Galactic Bill of Rights is constructed that satisfies the students. Using the procedure to amend the constitution under Article V, we add this document to our constitution. In a final meeting, the colonial groups compare their Galactic Bill of Rights to the U.S. Bill of Rights, listing similarities and differences.

All the pieces of this unit are saved for future portfolio use. I tried something different this year, a group practice portfolio at the end of our second trimester. Of special interest to me was the number of students who chose the constitution as evidence of one of the following attributes: creativity, problem-solving, ability to work in a group, read with understanding, or write clearly and concisely. See Appendix 7-10 for a brief description of group practice portfolios.

Personal journal entries reflect the involvement of the kids in this study:

I think space was an interesting thing to study. I learned a lot about space. It was very fun and if I had a chance to do this again I would almost definitely do it. I have had so much fun and been so interested my mom thinks I should be an astronaut when I grow up.

—Kara

This was the coolest and most fun unit I ever studied. My favorite part was making Jetsonland. It would really be hard to start up a space colony. I don't know how the patriots could agree on so many things. I learned a lot and the space bubble was rad.—Kendra

I think this was one of my favorite projects I've ever done. One of the best parts was making the people. As you know, I want to be an author when I grow up. I just thought of this person as one of my characters and set to work. It was really fun drawing the person and making a job description. My person was an author. But making the actual space colony was hard. We all had our own ideas. We finally decided we all could have a place. One of the hardest parts was making a name. We'd think up a good name and then one person would disagree. Our final name, only four of us liked. This was fun!—Caitlyn

I liked the space thing a lot. I cannot think of one thing I would change. I didn't know half the things we learned and, as you can probably guess, this was a big change for me. I realized I don't have to have everything my way. It won't kill me if I don't get everything exactly my way, and I don't have to own the world. I am

173

Welcome to Our Own Special World!

slowly getting over being so bossy and this was a big help. I learned how to work in a group successfully. I loved it!—Julie

I really liked learning about space. I also liked making our own Green Book. I liked learning what government does.—Andrew

Endnote

And so our constitution-in-space unit comes to a conclusion. We unplug the fan in the biosphere and watch it slowly deflate. The groups are reluctant to take down their colonial repositories and the kids resist taking spacekind career dolls home. If it weren't that we were really looking forward to learning about the experiences of people during the Civil War, we'd never let this unit end.

Appendix 7-1: Basic Assumptions Compiled About Living in Space

1. People and objects float in space since there is so little gravity. This "weightlessness" is one of the reasons many scientists support building colonies in space. Workers in space can build huge structures much more easily than on Earth because they don't have to overcome the forces of gravity.
2. Why not build colonies on existing planets? Venus and Mars lack some of the resources humans need. Mars has no atmosphere, and the surface temperature on Venus is too hot for humans to survive.
3. Why not build colonies on the moon? While small mining operations may be built on the moon, it is not the best site for large-scale colonization. One reason is the cost of getting supplies from the earth to the moon. Second, because of the moon's gravity, some of the same problems associated with building on Earth are also present on the moon. Finally, nights on the moon are two weeks long. These long periods of darkness require expensive energy sources.

4. The moon's surface has a wealth of natural resources: aluminum and titanium to provide lightweight but very strong building materials; oxygen for water and for breathing; and silicon, a basic element in glassmaking. Mining the moon for resources to build space colonies is inexpensive and efficient.

5. Our solar system is not dark, but full of sunlight. Energy from the sun can provide space colonies with endless cheap energy. Space stations can turn solar energy into power for electricity. Properly positioned mirrors can concentrate sunlight for manufacturing.

6. The most reasonable place to build the first space colony would be where gravity will not pull it out of place. Placing a colony in a stable orbit around the moon or sun, far enough away so that sunlight would not disappear during a solar eclipse, seems best.

7. A scientist who lived two hundred years ago, Joseph-Louis Lagrange, identified certain spots in space that he thought were stable. He said that if an object is placed in one of these spots, it will remain there forever. These points are named L-1 through L-5. Only points L-4 and L-5 are really appropriate for space colonization. Both points are located where the gravity of the sun, earth, and moon cancel one another out.

8. Scientists believe that at least ten thousand people have to live in the first space colony to make the colony economically successful. Crop, manufacturing, and recreation areas can be created to sustain people for the rest of their lives.

9. NASA has done extensive testing on weightlessness for human beings. Extended weightlessness has bad effects on the bones, muscles, and blood. Centrifugal force, the force that seems to push you away from the center when you are riding a carnival ride that whirls around in a circle, can be used to help colonists create a kind of gravity similar to earth's in their living areas. Rotating habitats approximately two times a minute can simulate earth's gravity.

10. Nitrogen, hydrogen, carbon, certain machines and equipment, medical supplies, and seeds for crops are all the

colonists need from Earth. Using elements mined from the moon, colonists will be able to create an earthlike environment, with lakes, fields, hills, and valleys.

11. The perfect mix of sunlight and moisture can be created to allow the colonists to grow a large amount of food in a small amount of space. Soybeans, wheat, rice, and other crops, as well as chickens, turkeys, and fish, provide a varied diet.

12. Special laboratories can be built that make use of the qualities of space that are difficult to achieve on Earth, such as the lack of gravity, extremely high/low temperatures, and strong radiation from the sun. Space also provides an almost perfect vacuum, a condition that is very expensive and very hard to duplicate on Earth.

13. Space colonists can build huge solar reflectors to beam the sun's energy down to Earth, eliminating the need for other energy sources that pollute Earth's atmosphere and providing abundant, inexpensive energy. These reflectors can provide the colonists with important income to continue enriching their life in space.

14. After the technology of building space colonies is perfected, larger settlements will be possible. Scientists have already sketched plans for colonies of ten million or more people. These colonies will be able to absorb the ever-increasing populations on Earth.

15. In the future of space colonization, mining can extend to the two moons of Mars, the moons of Jupiter and Saturn, and an asteroid belt located between the orbits of Mars and Jupiter. Carbon, nitrogen, and hydrogen, resources the first colonists will need to bring from earth, are found in rich deposits in the asteroid belt.

16. There may come a time when human beings won't be able to imagine not living in space. They will look upon Earth as "old-fashioned" and visit it like a museum, to trace their ancestors and to explore the history and culture of the early life of the human race (Laedlein, et al. 1980).

Appendix 7-2: Guided Fantasy Prompts

Close your eyes. Relax. Take a deep breath and let it out s-l-o-w-l-y. Come with me on an adventure. Climb into my space shuttle. It's warm and safe. Nothing can harm you in this marvelous vehicle!

We strap in, say farewell, and leave Earth behind. Although you aren't feeling any sensation of movement, you notice that we are soaring through the atmosphere, heading for deep space. Our target, L-4.

It only seems a moment and you've arrived! You've come home. You recognize this place. Slowly, you refamiliarize yourself with it. You are aware of the slight pull of centrifugal force as the spinning colony compensates for the lack of gravity. You have landed at the habitat. You recall when this was just a young pioneering colony.

Remember when you and your friends argued over the size of the colony? How big is it? What are some of the natural resources and features of this colony? Is the climate what you remembered? The citizens here call themselves spacekind. What do they wear? How do they look?

Let's go into the center of the city. What kind of transportation do we use? Did you notice what spacekind live in? Look at all the spacekind. What kind of work do they do? Have you seen any children?

It's time for us to return to the shuttle. Here we are, back on Earth. Slowly open your eyes when you are ready. Welcome back.

Appendix 7-3: Focus Questions for General Data Disc

Size/Physical Features: How big? Think about the number of people who will live in your community. Give the size in miles or meters or give a well-known reference (for example, "the size of Mercer Island"). Physical features include lakes, mountains, waterfalls, deserts, plains, hills, rivers, and islands. Create the habitat you would like to live in for a lifetime.

Climate: How hot does it get in your community? How cold? Does the wind blow? How hard? How much rainfall is there per year?

How much snow? Is your climate tropical, temperate, arid, or arctic? Decide and write it down.

"Extranatural" Resources: The resources aren't really natural because humans will have put them there. After a time, however, it will seem as though they've always been there. Think of trees, water, precious metals like gold and silver, mineral resources like copper, aluminum, and iron. Think of mining oxygen, hydrogen, and silicon. Consider the land, forests, mines, water, and energy of your colony.

Population: Scientists predict that the smallest population needed for a space colony is ten thousand people. Designs have already been created for space colonies of up to ten million people. Think of the size of your community and agree on a population that fits.

Chief Products: What is produced in your community to sell, trade, or use? While you may have many products, select the main ones to list on your disc. Consider your natural resources, climate, and physical features as you make these choices. Remember, your chief products affect the work people do in your community.

Appendix 7-4: Pool-and-Pick Decision Making

Pool

Begin with the section on size and physical features. Have the students individually write down on separate slips of paper each of their ideas for that particular section. After they read these ideas to one another, have them put all the slips into a "pool."

Pick

A student picks one idea that she or he likes from the pool and writes it on the disc. The next student picks one idea he or she likes for that same section and records it on the disc and so on until each group member has a turn.

Pool and Pick

Move to another section, such as climate. Repeat the process. Be sure each student writes down his or her ideas. If an idea is not on paper, it can't be considered. Continue with natural resources, population, and chief products. Encourage groups to refer to the overhead or the handout describing each section as they progress. (Most groups stop using the pool-and-pick method and begin cooperatively adding their ideas after one or two sections are completed.)

Appendix 7-5: Space Bubble (Biosphere)

Materials Needed

4 mm clear polyethylene sheeting. Use three rows 10′ by 25′.

Two rolls of 2″ duct tape. Need 75 feet for construction and extra for possible repairs.

Window fan, 14″ to 20″ square. Two or more speeds is desirable.

Old blankets or bedspreads to put under the bubble unless floor is carpeted.

Blankets, beach towels, or rugs to put on floor inside the bubble.

A large room (gym or multipurpose room) is needed to lay out the bubble pieces before taping begins.

Assembling the Bubble

Cut the plastic as shown in Figure 7-2, saving the top portion, which will be used later for the tube between the bubble and the fan.

Tape plastic together as shown in the drawing. Inflated, it looks like a pillow.

Make a tube of remaining plastic. The tube may be any length desired. Tape the plastic to the outside of the fan on all sides.

Cut a slit horizontally in the side of the bubble near the bottom. Tape the fan tube to the bubble. Placement of the fan and tube depends on what is convenient for your classroom.

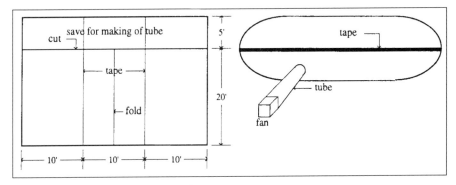

FIG. 7-2: *Space (Bubble) Biosphere Diagram*

Turn on the fan and inflate the bubble. To make a slit for the door, use scissors to cut a horizontal slit large enough for the tallest person to enter. Place tape on the edges of the slit for reinforcement.

Size of the Bubble

It is about 20′ by 15′, or you can adapt it to the size of your classroom. When inflated, the bubble is five and a half to six feet high. It will hold up to forty people, depending on the size of the individuals and the activity going on.

Helpful Hints for a Bubble in the Classroom

1. The fan remains on at all times, day and night.
2. The bubble is not airtight and was not meant to be.
3. If you use audiovisual equipment, a *small* slit at the bottom of the bubble where you want the cords to enter is sufficient. You won't need to tape it back together.
4. You can project images on the bubble walls themselves (gives a 3-D effect, sort of blurry) or tape a piece of clear white butcher paper on the outside of the bubble (images are clear if the lens is high quality).
5. If you choose to project images from outside the bubble, remember images will be reversed, so if that is a concern turn slides around.

6. With lights out, various colors can be projected on the bubble. You may use a color wheel or various colors of cellophane. Black lights may also be used for unusual effects and illusions.
7. Be sure to have your class determine rules for using the bubble, including personal behavior, guests, appropriate activities, and care and cleaning of the bubble.
8. Take off shoes before entering the bubble.
9. Two or three 2" by 10" pieces of duct tape will "close" the door of the bubble to allow for maximum inflation. Place the tape perpendicular to the door slit. Change as needed.
10. Less air will be lost at opening and closing times if the "door" is placed near the end where the fan is located and on the same side of the bubble as the fan.
11. Don't eat in the bubble. Crumbs and spills are difficult to handle.
12. Patch holes as soon as they are noticed. Patching on both sides is desirable.
13. Decide ahead of time how long to keep the bubble inflated. Two weeks is a long time.
14. After deflating the bubble, fold it into fourths, roll it up, and store it in a plastic garbage bag for use again next year.

If you plan to invite groups from other classrooms into the bubble, train "galactic guides" from your classroom to be the hosts.

Appendix 7-6: The Simplified Constitution of the United States of America

Preamble (Reasons for the Constitution)

We the People of the United States, in order to have a better government, to treat everyone fairly, to have a peaceful country, to defend the country from enemies, to live in a comfortable way, and to make sure people are free now and forever, make this Constitution for the United States of America.

Article I (The Legislative Branch)
Section 1 (Description)

This branch of the government, also called the Congress, shall make all the laws for the country. It shall have two parts or houses: the House of Representatives and the Senate.

Section 2 (House of Representatives)

Members of the House of Representatives shall be elected by the people for two years at a time (called a term). They need to be at least twenty-five years old and live in the state they are elected to represent. They must have been American citizens for at least seven years before they can be elected.

The number of representatives from each state is determined by its population. States with large populations get more representatives than states with small populations. Every ten years there will be an official counting (or census) of all the people to see how many representatives a state gets.

Section 3 (The Senate)

Each state elects only two senators. They serve six-year terms. Senators must be at least thirty years old and they must have been citizens of the United States for at least nine years. They must live in the state they represent.

The Vice President of the United States is in charge of the Senate. However, the Vice President can only vote in the Senate when there is a tie.

Sections 4–7 (Rules)

The Congress shall meet at least once every year, beginning on January 3. Each House shall take care of its own procedures and the behavior of its members. Members cannot be arrested (except for serious crimes) while attending sessions of their Houses, and they cannot be punished for anything they say while in speech or debate during the meetings. The government shall pay the members of the House and the Senate.

Proposed laws (bills) having to do with raising money must start in the House of Representatives. Bills approved by the House and the Senate must go to the President for approval. If the President does not approve, the bill goes back to the House and the Senate. If two thirds of each House approves, the bill becomes a law without the President's approval.

Sections 8–10 (Duties)

The Congress makes all laws having to do with money, such as taxes. The Congress also makes all trade laws, such as buying and selling things to other countries. The Congress coins (makes) money, runs the post office, and provides inventors with patents. The Congress can declare war. Congress provides for and maintains the military.

There are also things the Congress and the States cannot do, such as give royal titles, keep private armies, or use government money in secret.

Article II (The Executive Branch)
Section 1 (Description)

The President, the Vice President, and those who work under the President to help carry out the laws Congress passes are the executive branch of the government. Both the President and Vice President are elected to four-year terms. The President must have been born in the United States, be at least thirty-five years old, and have lived within the United States for at least fourteen years.

Sections 2–4 (Duties)

The President has many jobs, including carrying out the laws made by Congress, commanding the military, making treaties, appointing ambassadors and governmental leaders, and receiving ambassadors and leaders from other countries. The President must report to Congress on what the nation is doing. (The State of the Union address is given each year when Congress convenes.) The President may be removed from office (impeached) if he or she commits a crime against the government. The President also has the power to pardon federal criminals.

Article III (The Judicial Branch)
Section 1 (Description)

The judicial branch serves as the court system for the whole country (federal court system). The Supreme Court, the highest court in the nation, has the final say in all matters of law. Federal judges are not elected; they are appointed for life.

Section 2 (Cases to Be Heard; Jurisdiction)

The federal court system has the say in all cases involving this Constitution, laws made by Congress, and certain other types of cases involving people from different states.

Section 3 (Treason)

Treason is explained as the act of a U.S. citizen trying to overthrow the government. No one can be convicted of treason without the testimony of at least two witnesses or by public confession of the accused.

Article IV (The States)
Sections 1–4 (Rules About the States)

The states must accept one another's laws, records, and acts. When someone is visiting a state, he or she must be given the same rights as someone living in that state. Accused criminals can be sent back to the state where a crime was committed for trial by the governor of another state. New states may join the union. All states are protected from enemies by the United States government.

Article V (Amendments)

The Constitution can be changed (amended) with the cooperation of the Congress (House of Representatives and Senate) and the States.

Article VI (The Highest Law)

The Constitution, treaties, and laws made by Congress are higher than state laws. All lawmakers, both national and state, must take an oath or affirmation to support the Constitution. However, no religious test shall ever be required as a qualification for any office in the United States.

Article VII (Ratification)

This Constitution becomes law when nine of the thirteen states ratify (approve) it. Done in Convention, by the unanimous consent of the States present, the seventeenth day of September in the year of our Lord one thousand seven hundred and eighty-seven. The members present witnessed and signed the Constitution.

On June 21, 1788, New Hampshire became the ninth state to ratify the Constitution, and the Constitution became law.

Appendix 7-7: Constitutional Focus Questions

Preamble

What are the objectives of the constitution? What do its authors hope the constitution will achieve for the space nation and its citizens? Who are the authors and what authority do they have to write a constitution? Should the three basic functions of government be put together in one person or group, or should they be divided, with checks and balances?

Article I—The Legislative Branch

Sections 1–3

What is the lawmaking body? Will members of the lawmaking body be elected or appointed?

Sections 4–7

When will the lawmaking group meet? How many members need to be present to conduct business? How will members be punished for disorderly behavior? What records will the lawmaking body keep?

Are the records private or public? Do the lawmakers have any special rights? What is the process for making a law?

Sections 8–10

How will the election or appointment be handled? What qualifications must members have? What happens if a lawmaker is no longer able to perform the job? Should the lawmaking group have unlimited power? If not, which powers should the lawmaking group have?

Article II—The Executive Branch

Who will enforce the laws made by the lawmaking body? Will there be a chief of the space nation or a committee to run the space nation? How will the chief or committee be chosen? What powers will the chief or commitee have? Who is eligible to be the chief or on the committee? How can the chief or one or more committee members be removed from office?

Article III—The Judicial Branch

Who will decide disputes among the inhabitants? How will this judicial system be structured? What cases can the justices decide? What type of hearings will be held?

Articles IV–VII—The States, Amendments, the Highest Law, and Ratification

Can the space nation be enlarged? Can other colonies join? How will this be done? Will all inhabitants of the space nation have the same rights? How can the space nation's constitution be changed? What law is supreme? What process will make the drafted constitution apply to the space nation?

Appendix 7-8: Student Space Colony Constitution— The Constitution of Unerbobbia

Preamble

We, the Unerbobbians of Unerbobbia, in order to create a better colony, to treat everyone fairly, to defend the colony from enemies, to live in a comfortable way, and to ensure freedom now and forever, form this Constitution for the Unercolonies of Unerbobbia.

Article I
Section 1 (The Legislative Branch)
This branch of government, also called Unerlaw, shall make the laws for Unerbobbia. It will have two branches or huts: the Hut of Representatives and the Bobbia (Senate).

Section 2
Members of the Hut of Representatives shall be elected by the people for 3 years, 4 months, 13 days, 5 hours, and 8 minutes, 21 seconds at a time. They need to be $22\frac{1}{2}$ years 58 seconds old and they must have lived in the colony they represent. They must have been off earth for at least four years. The number of representatives are determined by the population of the colony. Every ten years there will be an official counting of representatives.

Section 3
Each colony shall have three Bobbians (senators). They shall serve seven years, one month and ninety days. Bobbians must be twenty-four years old. They need to have lived in the colony they represent.

Sections 4–7
The President of Unerbobbia is in charge of the Bobbia and the Hut of Representatives, known as the Unerlaw.

The Unerlaw must meet at least five times a year. Every member of the Hut or Bobbia is in charge of his/her/its own actions. The Bobbi-ment will pay members of the Unerlaw.

Any money or raising money related law must start in the Hut of Representatives. Laws by the Unerlaw must go to the President to be approved. If it is not, it is sent back to the Hut and Bobbia. If $\frac{2}{3}$ of the Unerlaw approves the law, it is automatically a new law in Unerbobbia.

Sections 8–10 (Duties)

The Unerlaw makes all laws. The Unerlaw also runs the Solar System Post Office and provides inventors with patents. Unerlaw can also declare war. Unerlaw will take care of the military. Unerlaw cannot appoint royal titles or use Unerbobbian money in secret.

Article II
Section 1 (The Executive Branch)

The President of Unerbobbia is elected by the popular vote every 4 years. To be the President of Unerbobbia, you must be a Unerbobbian citizen and be at least 30 years of age.

Sections 2–4 (Duties)

The president has the responsibilities to execute laws. He also has the power to run the space nation of Unerbobbia, make treaties, and appoint ambassadors and governmental leaders. The only way the president can be removed from office, is if the Unerlaw committee gets a 9 out of 10 vote against him. The president also has the power to pardon galactic criminals. The President can be elected for 2 terms maximum.

Article III
Section 1 (The Judicial Branch)

The court system serves as the department that decides what happens to criminals after they have committed a felony. Each Colony has an individual court but if the case is appealed, it goes to Unerbobbia Courthouse. The Unerbobbia Courthouse is located in the middle of Unerbobbia. There must be two sides to every case with a certified Prosecutor and Lawyer of Defense. The Court Justices are appointed by the President and are accepted by the lower Colony courts. The Justices must be at least 30 and a Unerbobbia citizen for 6 years before getting appointed. The terms are 50 years long and there will be three justices.

Section 2 (Cases to Be Heard—Jurisdiction)

If a case is appealed by a lower court and the Supreme Court does not accept the appeal, this Constitution will be referred to. If it is an

Inter-colony Crime, it will be worked out immediately by the Supreme Court. If a crime is committed Inter-Colony and it is appealed by the Defendant to the Supreme Court, this Constitution will be recalled. If the Justice cannot find any reason to keep prosecuting, the Defendant will be released but watched.

Section 3 (Treason)

If treason occurs, no one can override the government in any way. If someone is caught and convicted of a crime, and accused of treason they will be convicted of the crime and, if there were at least two witnesses, they also may be convicted of treason.

Section 4 (Rules)

A colony must accept each other's laws, records, and acts. When someone is visiting a colony, he/she must be given the same rights as someone living in that colony. Accused criminals can be sent back to the colony where a crime was committed for trial by the governor of another colony. New colonies may join the union. All colonies are protected from enemies by the Unerbobbia government.

Articles IV–VII (The Colonies)

A new colony can, by majority vote, join Unerbobbia. All life forms have the same rights as everyone else. The Constitution can only be changed if every citizen agrees on the changing by an 80% vote in agreement. This will help people to live in peace. We, the people, can and will establish this Constitution for Unerbobbia.

Signed on the fifth day of the second month of the 1997th year of the twentieth century, by these founding citizens: *[Signatures of twenty-four students from Mrs. Lindquist's Class of '97.]*

Terms used:

Unerlaw—Congress

Bobbia—Senate

Hut of Representatives—House of Representatives

190

Galactic Court—Supreme Court

Bobbi-ment—Government

Appendix 7-9: Simplified United States Bill of Rights

First Amendment

This amendment guarantees the rights of freedom of religion, freedom of speech, freedom of the press, freedom for people to get together peacefully, and freedom to send petitions to the government.

Second Amendment

This amendment states that in order to have a prepared military, people are guaranteed the right to keep and bear arms.

Third Amendment

This amendment states that the government cannot force the people to house and feed soldiers in their homes during times of peace.

Fourth Amendment

This amendment states that people, their homes, and their belongings are protected from unreasonable searches or seizures. Warrants may not be issued except upon probable cause and must specifically describe the place to be searched and the person or thing to be seized.

Fifth Amendment

This amendment guarantees a person accused of a serious crime the right to be charged by a grand jury. Persons cannot be forced to give evidence against themselves. If a person is found not guilty of a crime, he or she cannot be put on trial for the same crime again. People's lives, freedom, or property cannot be unfairly taken from them. The government must pay a person for any property it takes from them for public use.

Sixth Amendment

This amendment guarantees a speedy and public trial by an impartial jury if a person is accused of a crime. Accused persons have the right to be told what they are accused of. They have the right to a lawyer. They have a right to see and to question those people who accuse them of the crime.

Seventh Amendment

This amendment guarantees a trial by jury in civil cases (disputes between private parties or between the government and a private party).

Eighth Amendment

This amendment guarantees that excessive bail or excessive fines will not be imposed and that punishment will not be cruel and unusual.

Ninth Amendment

This amendment states that the people have other rights that are not stated here.

Tenth Amendment

This amendment states that the people have all the rights not given to the United States government or forbidden to state governments by the Constitution.

Appendix 7-10: Group Practice Portfolios

My students prepare portfolios of their work at the end of the school year. Working with their parents, they go on a "scavenger hunt" through the projects and products created throughout the year in search of evidence of learning. This style of portfolio presentation has been especially positive in home-school communications. Parents, as well as the kids, have an opportunity to evaluate the quality of the work accomplished over an extended period of time, note the various intelligences that have been tapped, and appreciate the diversity of learning that has occurred. I have found nothing better to help my students and their parents comprehend the depth and the integration of learning that occurs in my classroom. I am deeply indebted to Ruth Haynsworth of Providence, Rhode Island, for sharing her insights and her organization of portfolio scavenger hunts with me.

This year I tried something new. Picture my students sitting on the floor around our classroom with the products they had created during the Constitutional Visions unit as well as other projects during second trimester. From eight categories—social studies, science, reading, math, writing, problem-solving, creativity, and personal best—each child selected a product as evidence of learning in each of the categories. Filling out a personal reflection identifying the category and the product, the students stated why their choices showed evidence of learning. The conversations were so insightful as the students chose, discarded, or replaced one product with another, finding the perfect product to prove they had learned.

Then, in groups of four, the kids invited their parents to the classroom for a forty-five-minute presentation after school. The kids identified each category, shared their evidence, and told why they had chosen it. They frequently mentioned what they liked about the product or what they would change if they did it again. I was surprised to hear comments like ten-year-old Kendra's: "Good readers can paraphrase. I draw pictures after I read. Drawing is a form of paraphrasing. I have chosen my pop-up picture book about Harriet Tubman as evidence of my ability to read and comprehend because my pictures show that I know what happened during Harriet's life. I didn't know anything about her life before I read this biography, *Freedom Train.*"

The groups of four worked marvelously. By taking turns, first all doing the social studies category, then the science category, and so on, the students were able to support each other. No one had to talk for more than a few minutes at a time. As students took turns, parents were able to see a range of abilities, interests, and talents. They experienced the integrative nature of learning as they watched one child choose a product as evidence of reading ability, another choose the same product as evidence of ability to solve a problem, and a third child choose the same product as a sample of his creativity. Thinking on their feet, speaking effectively, organizing materials, and celebrating learning are some of the attributes of this kind of portfolio practice. I also think this particular kind of event builds a network of support for our kids and our schools. It affirms learning in a very special and powerful way.

I will still do my end-of-the-year portfolio scavenger hunt. But I will continue to include this practice portfolio at the end of second trimester. It makes learning important. It's a way that works.

Bibliography for the Constitution and Space

Books, Periodicals, Videos, Filmstrips

ARMBRUSTER, ANN, and ELIZABETH A. TAYLOR. 1990. *Astronaut Training*. New York: Franklin Watts. A good book for those kids who decide they want to be astronauts. Gives a clear picture of the job and responsibilities. Also provides addresses kids can write to for further information and suggests places to visit to learn more.

Aviation for the Elementary Level. Wichita, KS: Raytheon Aircraft Company. This is the best buy in town. In addition to excellent resources for lessons on powered flight ranging from an extensive time line to hands-on science experiments on the forces of flight to careers in the air, complete directions for the classroom "bubble" are given. (Aviation Education Dept., Dept. 892, 9709 E. Central, Wichita, KS 67206)

BEASANT, PAM. 1992. *1000 Facts About Space*. New York: Scholastic. An inexpensive paperback, this book is a catch-all of everything you wanted to know about space and didn't know enough to ask. Good resource for having kids create a believe-it-or-not book of facts about space of their own.

BOYNE, WALTER J. 1987. *The Smithsonian Book of Flight for Young People*. Washington, DC: Smithsonian Books. A basic reference book for students and their teachers regarding all aspects of flight, including colonizing space.

CROSS, WILBUR, and SUSANNA CROSS. 1985. *Space Shuttle*. Chicago: Children's Press. Discusses the history and development of the space shuttle, and how the "opening up" of space has affected every area of our lives. The final chapter on the future is especially interesting to budding space colonists.

ECO, UMBERTO, and EUGENIO CARMI. 1989. *The Three Astronauts*. San Diego: Harcourt Brace Jovanovich. A picture book that sets the tone for a kind and cooperative adventure in space, this story captures the way I want my kids to behave in space.

FISHER, LEONARD EVERETT. 1992. *Galileo*. New York: Macmillan. A dark and dense presentation of Galileo's life, this picture book provides a startling contrast to Peter Sis's interpretation of the same man and period in history.

FRITZ, JEAN. 1987. *Shh! We're Writing the Constitution*. New York: G. P. Putnam's Sons. Describes, in language kids understand, how the Constitution came to be written and ratified.

KERROD, ROBIN. 1984. *Living in Space*. Vero Beach, FL: Rourke Enterprises. Brief text and illustrations present the development of space travel from the launching of the first rockets and satellites to the space shuttle, which could make living and working in space a common experience in the near future.

———. 1989. *Out in Space*. New York: Warwick. Easily accessible information accompanied by simple hands-on experiments kids can do to simulate some of the challenges of living in space. Excellent glossary of terms used in space exploration.

KEY, ALEXANDER. 1965. *The Forgotten Door*. New York: Scholastic. I always have my kids read this chapter book before we begin the space unit since it provides an alternative view of beings from space—this one from a gentle and wise boy.

KNIGHT, DAVID D. 1977. *Colonies in Orbit: The Coming Age of Human Settlements in Space*. New York: William Morrow. Little has been written for juveniles on space colonization since the 1970s. I still use this book because the various schemes discussed by scientists for building an artificial satellite are as viable today as they were twenty some years ago. Public libraries tend to keep books this dated for young readers.

LAEDLEIN, JOHN, et al. 1980. *Colonies in Space*. Madison, WI: Knowledge Unlimited. A filmstrip with a script, this resource provides some excellent information about living in space. Even though it is dated, when it is combined with the video *Living in Space: The Countdown Has Begun*, the kids get a comprehensive overview of scientific thought about colonizing space.

LEEDY, LOREEN. 1993. *Postcards from Pluto: A Tour of the Solar System*. New York: Scholastic. A quick and easy paperback for all readers. I use this book to introduce postcards from space. My students create and write a postcard from their colony in space on their Constitution Day.

Living and Working in Space: The Countdown Has Begun. 1993. Los Angeles: FASE Productions. An excellent PBS video offering dozens of interviews with today's space professionals and narrated in an engaging way. (Contact PBS Video 800-424-7963.)

NASA. *The Sky as Your Classroom.* Houston: NASA/AESP. A teacher's aerospace workshop resource book, providing helpful information for teachers and students alike. (NASA/Johnson Space Center, Teacher Resource Center, Mail Code AP2, 2101 NASA Road 1, Houston, TX 77058-3696.)

POGUE, WILLIAM R. 1991. *How Do You Go to the Bathroom in Space?* New York: Tom Doherty. All the answers to all the questions anyone has about living in space, provided by an astronaut who spent eighty-four days in space. Cartoon drawings make this a fun and informational book.

POTTS, JODY. 1994. *Adventure Tales of America: An Illustrated History of the United States, 1492–1877.* Dallas: Signal Media. In this textbook for middle school students written by a specialist in left brain/right brain learning techniques, history is combined with highly graphic illustrations. An excellent resource for teachers and kids.

RIDE, SALLY, and SUSAN OKIE. 1986. *To Space and Back.* New York: Lothrop, Lee & Shepard. An easy-to-read introduction to living and working in space accompanied by highly informative photographs of astronauts in space.

RIDE, SALLY, and TAM O'SHAUGHNESSY. 1994. *The Third Planet: Exploring the Earth from Space.* New York: Crown. Another perspective, this time Earth from space, rather than space from Earth. This book helps me get the kids "into another space."

ROBINSON, GEORGE S. 1989. "Re-Examining Our Constitutional Heritage." *High Technology Law Journal* 3:33. An essay by one of the nation's leading lawyers in astrojurisprudence.

SHAYLER, DAVID. 1994. *Inside Outside Space.* New York: Random House. An easy-to-read compilation of space facts with a brief section on living in space.

SIS, PETER. 1996. *Starry Messenger.* New York: Farrar, Straus & Giroux. This fascinating picture book tells the story of Galileo in a way unique to

Peter Sis. As with a good painting, the reader can return to this book many times and find something not seen before, something to marvel at again. Students find it interesting to compare this presentation of Galileo's life to Leonard Fisher's picture book on the same man.

VOGT, GREGORY. 1987. *Space Walking.* New York: Franklin Watts. Text and photographs inform the reader of the challenges of working in space and the ways science on earth is trying to enhance the pros and reduce the cons. Provides factual information for future space colonists.

WALSH, JILL PATTON. 1982. *The Green Book.* New York: Farrar, Straus & Giroux. One of my favorite read-alouds about exploration and discovery, this time about the future. It is the story of the last spaceship to leave an ailing earth. The families on board were chosen for their talents and skills, which are soon traded and bartered when they reach their new home. Children teach the community what really matters. A sparse, compelling story, this book ignites the imagination and encourages fledgling writers.

WEST, ROBIN. 1987. *Far Out!* Minneapolis: Carolrhoda. A do-it-yourself instruction book for five- to ten-year-olds about creating a star world of critters, vehicles, and domiciles using common household materials. Stimulates thinking among kids to create a three-dimensional model of a "place in space."

Web Sites:

http://members.aol.com/oscarcombs/spacesetl.htm#advantages (Frequently asked questions [FAQs] about living in space, answered in a straightforward manner. The information seems accurate and current to me.)

http://www.millennial.org/

http://www.nas.nasa.gov/NAS/SpaceSettlement

http://www.astro.nwu.edu/lentz/space/ssi/home-ssi.html

http://www.nas.nasa.gov/NAS/S/SpaceSettlement/

General References

BURKE, KAY. 1994. *How to Assess Authentic Learning.* Palatine, IL: IRI/Skylight Publishing, Inc.

CAMPBELL, BRUCE. 1994. *The Multiple Intelligences Handbook: Lesson Plans and More* . . . Stanwood, WA: Campbell & Associates.

CAWELTI, GORDON, ed. 1995. *Handbook of Research on Improving Student Instruction.* Arlington, VA: Educational Research Service.

DEBONO, E. 1992. *Serious Creativity.* New York: HarperCollins.

DORRIS, MICHAEL. 1992. *Morning Girl.* New York: Bantam Doubleday Dell.

EVERETT, GWEN. Illustrated by Jacob Lawrence. 1993. *John Brown: One Man Against Slavery.* New York: Rizzoli.

FAIRFAX, BARBARA, and ADELA GARCIA. 1992. *Read! Write! Publish!: Making Books in the Classroom.* Cypress, CA: Creative Teaching Press, Inc.

GARDNER, HOWARD. 1985. *Frames of Mind.* New York: Basic.

GAUCH, PATRICIA LEE. 1975. *Thunder at Gettysburg.* New York: Bantam Doubleday Dell.

GREGORY, KRISTIANA. 1996. *The Winter of the Red Snow.* New York: Scholastic.

HAMMOND-BERNSON, MARY, ed. 1988. *China Mosaic: Multidisciplinary Units for the Middle Grades.* Olympia, WA: Office of the Superintendent of Public Instruction.

HOWARD, GARY. 1990. *REACH Training Materials.* Seattle, WA: The REACH Center.

IRVINE, JOAN. 1987. *How to Make Pop-ups*. New York: Beech Tree.

JAROLIMEK, JOHN, and WALTER C. PARKER. 1993. *Social Studies in Elementary Education*, 9th ed. New York: Macmillan.

LINCOLN, ABRAHAM. Illustrated by Michael McCurdy. 1995. *The Gettysburg Address*. Boston: Houghton Mifflin.

LINDQUIST, TARRY. 1995. *Seeing the Whole Through Social Studies*. Portsmouth, NH: Heinemann.

———. 1996. *Practical Strategies for Creating an Outstanding Fifth Grade Program: A Resource Handbook*. Bellevue, WA: Bureau of Education and Research.

MURPHY, JIM. 1990. *The Boys' War: Confederate and Union Soldiers Talk About the Civil War*. New York: Scholastic.

NATIONAL COUNCIL FOR THE SOCIAL STUDIES. 1994. *Curriculum Standards for Social Studies: Expectations of Excellence*. Washington, DC: National Council for the Social Studies.

PARKS, SANDRA, and HOWARD BLACK. 1990. *Organizing Thinking*. Pacific Grove, CA: Critical Thinking Press & Software.